LIFE ON THE OLD PLANTATION

IN ANTE BELLUM DAYS

OR

A Story Based On Facts

LIFE ON THE OLD PLANTATION

IN ANTE BELLUM DAYS

OR

A Story Based On Facts

BY

REV .I.E. LOWERY

With Brief Sketch of the Author by the Late Rev. J. Wofford White of the south caroline confer-ence, Methodist Episcopal Church

AND

An Appendix

KALPAZ

ISBN: 978-93-5128-684-4

First Published in 1911
Indian Reprint in 2017

Published by

Kalpaz Publications
C-30, Satyawati Nagar,
Delhi – 110052
E-mail: kalpaz@hotmail.com
Website: kalpazpublications.com
Ph.: +91-9212142040

"Backward, turn backward, O Time in your flight;
Make me a child again just for tonight."

MEMORIES.

O mystic Land of Smiles and Tears,
  O Land that Was and Is,
Alone—unchanging with the years—
  The Land of Memories.

—John Trotwood Moore.

CONTENTS

PART SECOND

APPENDIX

SIGNS OF A BETTER DAY FOR THE NEGRO IN THE SOUTH

By I. E. Lowery

I.

Introduction.

II.

White Patrons of Negro Business Enterprises.

III.

White Contributors Toward the Building of Negro Churches.

IV.

White Contributors Toward the Building of Negro Churches.—Continued.

PREFACE

I have no apology to make, and no excuse to offer for writing this book—"Life on the Old Plantation in Ante-Bellum Days." It is not the result of vanity, neither is it a desire for notoriety, that prompted me to write it. No, my reasons are higher, and my purposes are nobler. My only desire has been to do good. The religious element runs through the entire story.

It has been a work of faith and a labor of love to me. I cannot express the pleasure I have had in sitting down, and recalling the incidents of my childhood and youth. In doing so, it has enabled me to live my life over again. I only hope that the reader will experience something of the same pleasure in reading the book that I have had in writing it.

The "Brief Sketches of the Author" were written just twenty years ago by the late Rev. J. Wofford White. He was a colored man, and a close friend of mine, and was born and reared in the same neighborhood with myself. These sketches were printed in *The Christian Witness*, a Boston (Mass.) newspaper, and were clipped and carefully pasted in my scrapbook. I republish them in this connection without changing a single word. I would ask the reader to peruse them carefully, and compare them with Chapter XI, entitled "Little Jimmie, the Mail Boy," and note the similarity of characters.

I have written this book because there is no other work in existence just like it. No author, white or colored, so far as I know, has traversed, or attempted to traverse, the literary path which I presume to have trodden in writing this book. We are now about forty-five years away from the last days of slavery and the first days of freedom, and the people who have any personal knowledge of those days are rapidly crossing the mystic river, and entering the land that knows no shadows; and soon, there will not be one left to tell the story. And it is the author's thought that a record of the better life of those days should be left for the good of the future generations of this beautiful southland. Others have written of the evil side of those days, but the author felt it to be his mission to write of the better side.

Before the war, the relation that existed between the master and his slaves was, in most cases, one of tenderness and affection. There was a mutual attachment between them, which has commanded the admiration of the world. But since the war, an estrangement between the colored and the white races has sprung up, which has resulted in a feeling of intense bitterness and alienation. But I am glad to say that things are now taking a turn for the better. I can see signs of a better day ahead; and if this book should, in any way, contribute to, and help on this much desired day, the author will be satisfied.

I conclude this preface with the following clipping:

WANT TO HONOR OLD SLAVES.

An appeal to erect a monument to the former slaves of the South was issued in New Orleans a few days ago from the headquarters of the United Confederate Veterans by Gen. George W. Gordon, commander-in-chief of the veterans.

The appeal is in the form of a general order, which quotes the resolutions favoring such a monument adopted at the Birmingham reunion in 1908, and adds:

"Only those familiar with the beautiful patriarchial life on the Southern plantations previous to 1865 know of the devotions of the slaves to their owners and the children of the family. They were raised more like members of a large household.

"The children of the owners and the slaves associated most intimately together, and enjoyed alike the pleasure of the home, all receiving the care and attention of the heads of the family, who had a feeling of tender affections for these departments."

The devotion of these slaves during war time in caring for the plantations, in sharing dangers at the front and nursing the wounded is noted, and the order concludes with an appeal to the U. C. V., the U. D. C., the U. S. C. V., and the C. S. M. A., to see "that some evidence is given to the world of their appreciation of the faithfulness and affection of this devoted people."

I. E. LOWERY.

Columbia, S. C., September 13, 1910.

BRIEF SKETCHES OF THE AUTHOR.

I.

BY THE LATE REV. J. WOFFORD WHITE.

When one has accomplished something of good for his fellowman, and performed work worthy of praise, people become interested not only in what he has done, but also in the history of the person himself. As fulsome praise is invidious, and heartless flattery no less damaging than unjust, we shall not make the mistake of committing the blunder of doing either, but shall state the facts as they exist.

The Rev. Irving E. Lowery, A. M., was born in the County of Sumter, State of South Carolina, September 16th, 1850, and is, therefore, 37 years old. His parents were born slaves; it was in this condition, too, that he came into this world. His father lives today [He has since died—THE AUTHOR] at the ripe age of almost four-score years. He has been known always as a man of integrity, strict honesty, and possessed of much energy and industry, and withal a man of much natural ability. Long before the war, by economy and frugality, he had saved enough in hard-earned wages to purchase his own freedom. He succeeded also in purchasing the freedom of his mother, and when Abraham Lincoln issued the famous Emancipation Proclamation he was making herculean efforts to purchase his wife. Under the new order of things, by dint of perseverance and hard labor by night as well as day, he managed with shrewdness to secure an excellent farm, and although today the hoar-frost of seventy-eight winters is clearly observable, he superintends his business, is observant of passing events, and takes a lively interest in the questions of the day. The mother has been noted always for her modesty, piety, and Christ-like demeanor. To her the children are indebted for all the home training they received that pertains to the Christian life.

Years ago, when the subject of these sketches was a mere boy, this pious mother, without a dream of freedom, with faith in the God she served, prayed that He would call one of her sons to be a preacher of the Gospel, which then meant to be an exhorter or class-leader. "Only this and nothing more." Wonderful as mysterious are the ways of God! Long years afterward that mother's prayers were signally answered in a way wonderful to speak of—a way she could not have appreciated at the time the prayers were offered. It is an example worthy of being followed by all Christian parents, who should unfalteringly commit their children by faith and prayer to the Lord. After they are dead, in answer to the prayers on behalf of their children, God will in some way bring about the desired results. How these prayers were answered will be related further on.

Brother Lowery had better advantages than most of the boys on the plantation. Being of a lively, quick and sprightly disposition, his owner took him "into the house" when he was quite young. In the same room, on a little pallet, he slept with his master and wife. He made the fires in the early winter mornings, blew the signal at the break of day for the feeding of the horses and beginning the preparations for the labor of the day. As the master was a Methodist of the old-fashioned type common "in ye olden time," there was a family altar in that house, and this little slave boy was one who bowed at it in devotion. A little pony for his exclusive use to ride for mail and do errands, was furnished him. In going to the county-seat on business, or when visiting alone or with his family, this boy was invariably the companion of his master; thus he saw more than the other boys, came in contact with more people, obtained a better knowledge of men and things, and as a result, he became more observant, more inquisitive, and more intelligent. Thus, even in a condition of abject thralldom, God was making the wrath of men to praise

Him by causing them thus to sow the seeds of usefulness in the heart of one whom He determined, in answer to the prayers of a pious mother, to lead into paths of holiness, usefulness and peace, and to become a preacher of the Gospel of our Lord and Savior Jesus Christ. As to church privileges, he had but few, although the best of such as were allowed slaves. Anon he was permitted to go to public service at the church, but more frequently the slaves were gathered together in old master's yard, and some exhorter or leader was allowed to come, under the surveillance of a white man, lest something insurrectionary be said—and conduct a service of prayer and praise.

As this was the limit of their liberty to worship, it is not to be wondered at that they entered into their services with a zeal and fervency, and to this day it is said of the negro that they pray more, and naturally sing better, than any other race. We say nothing of slavery, since it is accursed of God and man, but even with the best possible circumstances under such a condition and environment, no one could become efficient and useful in the highest sense of the term. That system had no elements to draw out the best in any one, be he master or slave. It was calculated to bring out the worst in both, and develop it to an unlimited degree. This proved to be the invariable result. True, many were saved, and we know of many good people that lived in those days, but it must be remembered that God's love is so far-reaching that it accomplishes what is impossible to man. Of itself, what did slavery do for any? What did it do for our brother? Absolutely nothing. Dear readers, when the morning of January first, 1863, dawned upon this fair but then blighted land, and the first ray of hope—the Proclamation of Emancipation—burst forth from a leaden sky, he who has ere this become a familiar name in your household, had not learned his alphabet, was in blissful ignorance of his high calling, had dreamed naught else than a life of slavery; in this condition because of his training from infancy, he was contented to live, and worse than all, he had not tasted of Jesus's blood that purifies our sinful hearts.

Brief Sketches of the Author.

II.

More than two years passed after that immortal document had been made public. Not till the South had stacked arms at Appomattox, and agents of the Government sent to every plantation to effect a legal contract between master and slaves, did the great mass of negroes learn that they were indeed freed men. When this was thoroughly understood, old men and women jumped for joy, young men and maidens clapped their hands and shouted. The old masters submitted, apparently, to the new order of things. When the agent came around, Brother Lowery was then a boy in his teens, and he signed the contract to remain that year.

He continued, till one day he was approached by his old master's son with a whip in one hand and a gun in the other. Without any provocation, he began to thrash the servants unmercifully. Seeing that his turn would soon come, he said to a companion, older than himself, "I will not stand this; I will go to Sumter and complain to the Provost Marshal." He leaped over the fence, and into the dense forest ran, followed by the friend referred to. Night was fast approaching; they wandered and traveled through swamps, and waded branches, till, after a ramble of fifteen miles, they got to the railroad that runs by the county-seat. Here they stopped to rest, as it was late at night, with the damp earth for a bed and the heavens for a covering. When the sun arose they aroused themselves, and shivering with cold, affrighted and hungry, they hurried toward their destination, about twenty miles away. They reached the place, inquired their way to the proper office, and were ushered into the presence of the Provost Marshal. Their complaint in simple language was made.

This was Brother Lowery's first public address, which was a statement of the grievances he had been made to suffer. After he had finished the reaction came, and the untutored youth melted into tears. The redress he sought was granted in part. A writ from this office turned him over to the custody of his father. With him, on a rented farm, he labored. At the end of that year the family was all reunited. In the year 1866, through the philanthropy of an educational society of New England, a free school, the first ever opened in that community for negroes, began its session. At the age of sixteen he was entered by his father and began the arduous task of mastering the alphabet after the manner pursued by teachers in ye olden time. He readily took to learning, and very soon was reading. His hunger for knowledge became intense. His father, according to his training, thought that work stood first in importance, and schooling was something to attend when farm work was over. This doctrine was very distasteful to one who had begun to drink from the fount of knowledge, so he ran away from his father, hired his time to work on the railroad; but the father, with an eye to business, waited patiently till the month was ended, was promptly on hand when the pay-train arrived and claimed the wages of his son—he being a minor. When the youth realized that thus it would be at the end of each succeeding month, he willingly returned to the home of his father.

The father, recognizing the exceeding anxiousness of the son to become educated, concluded to send him to school. As this stage marks the most important change in his life, pardon a little digression.

In 1865 the Rev. Timothy W. Lewis was sent to South Carolina to reorganize the Methodist Episcopal Church. He was soon strengthened by the Rev. A. Webster, D. D., recently deceased. Baker's Institute was established in Charleston for the training of young men for the ministry. One of the first to enter it was a brother full of zeal and the Holy Ghost. This brother belonged to the same community wherein lived Brother Lowery, and was widely known for his piety, having managed, with great secrecy, to obtain a fair knowledge of English branches. He spent one year at this institute. As the field was white and but few laborers, he was sent out to gather the people and assist in the organization of the church. This brother swayed great influence over the old, and especially the young. Among the young men who frequented the church under his ministry was the subject of our sketch.

Just about the time his father concluded to give every available advantage to enable him to prosecute his studies, he was happily converted under the pastorate of the sainted Joseph White, the brother referred to above. He joined the Methodist Episcopal Church in the year 1867. His conversion was sound and thorough, and although he hesitated to obey, he felt the irresistible call of God to preach the gospel of His Son. Thus the mother's prayers offered years before, when her son was a boy, were most singularly answered in the conversion of this son, and his being called to the ministry. He was licensed to exhort in the year 1868, and as the way was opened, he was directed by his pastor to Baker's Institute, which he entered and remained two years—1868 and 1869. He was the first student that registered at Claflin University. This was October, 1869.

There he continued till the latter part of 1870. In December of that year he was made a local preacher, joined the South Carolina Conference, was ordained deacon by Bishop Simpson and stationed by him at Cheraw. He remained there two years; he was then, at the beginning of 1873, sent to Columbia, where he remained till August. He then went to Wilbraham, Mass., to complete his education in the Wesleyan Academy, then under the presidency of Rev. Dr. Cooke. In the spring of 1874 he completely broke down in health and was forced to return home for the year. Influences, strong and powerful, were brought forward to induce him to enter politics. He was offered the nomination for School Commissioner, then equivalent to an election. Although the temptation was seductive, the inducements great and offers flattering, he turned neither to the right nor the left. He commanded Satan to get behind him, and he was obeyed, for the weakest Christian is stronger than the devil, because God dwelleth in him. Until the meeting of the Conference in January, 1875, he taught school in Sumter and was principal of the high school. It was here that he met the young lady who afterward became his wife. She is of noble and pious parentage, well educated, and, from peculiar advantages, was reared in the best colored society and influences in Charleston. It is a blessed union to both, and much of Brother Lowery's success in the ministry is due to the industry, energy and helpfulness of his wife. Five children enliven the interest of their home life, and they are carefully instructed in the way of life by their parents. Theirs is a model, Christian home, where the family Bible occupies a conspicuous place, and wherein is an altar erected to the Lord of Hosts, around which, twice a day—morning and evening—the family gather for worship, prayer and praise.

Brief Sketches of the Author.

III.

Rev. I. E. Lowery commenced again his active work in the ministry in the year 1875, soon after his return from Wesleyan Academy. He was appointed to Summerville by Bishop Wiley, an appointment high in grade, both because of the intelligence of the local membership and of its proximity to Charleston, many of whose best citizens, both white and colored, own homes and spend the summer there. With satisfaction to the people he remained there two years, and was by Bishop Harris appointed to the station of Greenville, with a membership of about 700, whose acquirements socially, intellectually and religiously are equal to that of any membership of any community or city in the State.

Soon after this young brother's arrival at his new field of labor he discovered that the people he was to serve were not only religious, but were Christians of a very pronounced and advanced type, many of whom were blessed with the grace of sanctification. Such openly professed, and, better still, lived it.

The Rev. True Whittier is one of the noble band of Christian missionaries that came to the South after the war. He was zealous for the Master. He preached sanctification all over the upper part of the State, where he served as presiding elder, and as a result numbers sought till they found full peace and cleansing of heart.

Greenville, of which we now write, was the principal hot-bed of this phase of Christian experience. Many here had enjoyed this fullness long before Brother Whittier's time, but they did not proclaim it as a distinct blessing. It is possible that they knew it not. He preached it, it was believed and many experienced it. This was the condition of the church when Brother Lowery took charge. He had not up to this time given much thought to this subject. Now he was made to face it. What could he do with a membership largely in advance of him in Christian experience? You can imagine the answer to such an inquiry more easily than it can be given. What did he do? He did what all ought to do who have not yet received it. Confessed his lack in that experience, earnestly solicited the prayers of the faithful, sought by meditation, prayer and faith until he found to his joy the blessed experience of sanctification, a second, separate and distinctly different blessing to that experienced in regeneration. He began then to preach as never before. His pulpit efforts were filled with a holy unction. Hitherto he had with all faithfulness preached the gospel, but now he preached a full gospel. While he does not make the subject a specialty, yet he hesitates not in claiming it as his own experience, and proclaiming the necessity of this experience not only to complete that of all Christians, but until it is sought and found the whole duty is not performed, requirements of spiritual life are not met, the danger line still in sight, and indeed not passed; for sanctification means, if anything, not only the pardon of sins, assurance and the other divine evidences of acceptance; it includes also the idea of the change in our nature of a proneness, inclination or natural bent to do evil, to a proneness or natural bent in us to do that only which pleases God. From the time of his experience of sanctification he has been, and is today, a different preacher altogether. The change is almost as marked between sanctification and regeneration as that between the highest type of moral living and regeneration. For three full years to an ever-increasing congregation and membership, he acceptably served the church at Greenville. It was with greatest reluctance that the people gave him up.

By Bishop Simpson, in the year 1880, he was appointed to Wesley, one of the three important stations in the city of Charleston. Under him the membership grew rapidly. Here he remained three years, full of labors for the Master, and when he was moved by expiration of the time-limit, he carried with him the good wishes of the membership of the church he had served so faithfully and well. Recently he visited Charleston, and as an illustration of the hold he has on the people, the church was crowded to overflowing to hear his sermons, and by careful computation 1,200 came to hear his lecture, "The Twenty Years' Progress of the Colored Race." Bishop Merrill then appointed him to Cheraw, his first appointment—an illustration of the theory of the eternal cycle that brings things back to the same condition of former times. The people were jubilant over the appointment. They received their old pastor with open hearts. Here he remained three years. Here he was again wonderfully blessed of the Lord. The charge prospered beyond that of any administration since he had left there years before. Here he and his family were bereaved of the favorite of the house—a bright 2-year-old boy—who departed this life and took up residence in Zion, city of our God. How this bereavement tried their souls! Other than prayerful meditation and resignation, two incidents were providentially sent as solaces. One in the person of the minister who conducted the burial services, who selected as a text these beautiful words, "My Beloved is Gone Down Into His Garden to Gather Lilies."—*Song of Solomon.* Such suggestive words were to them fraught with the fragrance of heaven. Ever after, in thinking of their little boy, these words loom uppermost in their minds. The other was from the pen of Bishop Foster, while on the Red Sea, homeward bound. When as a picture there loomed up before him all of his life's work and experience as a minister, he portrayed in graphic style his trials, struggles and the loss of a child, the first of that kind experienced by the young itinerant (himself), etc., which was almost an exact representation of the feelings and experiences of this family. To them this article was a message of condolence divinely sent. After serving a full Methodistic term here, he was appointed by Bishop Andrews to his present place of labor, Aiken, S. C., which, because of the peculiar circumstances surrounding it, is the most important appointment in the Conference at the present time.

Brother Lowery is tall and of commanding appearance. Suave in manner, quiet in disposition and devotional. His sermons are models of pulpit preparation. His style is more of the exposito-textual than that of the topical. He throws his whole soul into the delivery of a sermon, and not unfrequently somebody is either converted or so deeply impressed that conversion follows as a result of his powerful appeals.

In recent years he has developed taste of a literary nature. His papers in the columns of *The Witness* are widely read, and the readers of that journal have formed their own opinions as to their merits.

Twice has he been named as anniversary orator at Claflin University, and twice he has honored the occasion by efforts that surpassed even the expectations of his friends. He never sought nor desired it, yet the university has honored itself by conferring the degree A. M. upon him. If a degree is a recognition of worth, then it has been worthily bestowed in this instance. He is, however, that same modest, unassuming preacher of the gospel.

As a writer, he is painstaking, careful, scrutinizing. As a student, he is methodical, discriminating, industrious. As a preacher, he is forcible, logical, convincing. As a worker, he is indefatigable, energetic, pushing. As a financier, he is successful and skillful. As a Christian, he is sympathetic, consistent and spiritually-minded. God helping, we predict for him a career of usefulness to the church, his fellow men and the cause of Christ.

CHAPTER I.

THE OLD PLANTATION.

At a point about eight miles southeast of Mayesville, S. C., and about the same distance southwest of Lynchburg, is a settlement known as "Shiloh." There was a church located there which was called "the Shiloh Church"; hence the settlement took its name from the church. It was a Methodist Church, and belonged to that denomination known as the Methodist Episcopal Church, South. Not far from the church was a store owned by a man whose name was Chris. Player. Mr. Player kept the postoffice, and here the planters for miles around got their mail. It was a convenient place for a church and also for the store and postoffice, for they were located near where the public road forked at two places.

Just about two miles from this church, due north across the swamp, called Pudden Swamp, was the plantation which forms the scene of my story. I do not know the number of acres this farm contained (that is a matter of little consequence any way), but suffice it to say that it was a good sized plantation.

But how shall I begin to describe this wonderful old plantation? As I write the scene comes fresh before my vision. I imagine I can see the old farm house, where the white folks lived, nestled in the midst of a clump of stately old water oaks. There was a front and back piazza and there was a brick chimney at each end. It was a one-story building, with an ell running back, in which was located the dining room. About thirty feet east of the building was the kitchen, and about the same distance in the rear of the dining room stood the smoke-house and the store-room. That smoke-house was never without meat and lard, and that store-room contained barrels of flour, barrels of sugar, barrels of molasses and sacks of coffee from one year to another. And the corn, oh, there was no end to that. There were several barns, some big and some little, but when the corn was gathered and the "corn-shucking" was over and the crop was housed, the barns were full to overflowing. They would remind one of Pharaoh's barns in Egypt at the end of the seven years of plenty. There was very little cotton raised on that plantation in those days. Four or six bales were considered a good crop. But the corn, peas, potatoes, hogs, cattle, sheep and goats, there was no end to these. It was a rare thing to buy anything to eat on that plantation save sugar and coffee. Shoes were bought, but the clothing for the white folks and the slaves was made at home. It was the good old "homespun." On rainy days, when it was too wet to do outdoor work, the men and boys got out corn, as they said in plantation language, for the mill, while the women and girls carded and spun cotton and wool. A task of so many hanks of yarn was given them for a day's work, which was a reasonable task, and when it was finished they carded and spun for themselves. They more or less completed their tasks before night, and by working after night they were enabled to do almost as much for themselves as they did for the white folks during the day. The weaving was almost invariably done by the young white ladies, or by some one of the servant girls who was taught especially to do it. Thus everybody on the place was kept well clothed, both the white folks and the slaves. That which the slave women carded and spun at night was their own, and they usually hired their young missus, or some other white woman of the neighborhood, to weave it into cloth for them, and thus they always had good, clean clothing for Sunday wear, so that they could go to "meetin'" without embarrassment.

On the east side of the white folks' house was the orchard. It occupied a space of about five or six acres and contained a large number of fruit trees of every description. There could be found the apple in variety, the peach, the pear, the apricot and the plum. On the west side was a large vegetable garden, which contained, in addition to the supply of vegetables for the table, several varieties of grapes. The arbors built for these grapes were large, strong and well cared for. And the slaves got their portion of all these delicious fruits. Of course, they were not allowed to steal them (but this does not signify that they never resorted to this method of obtaining fruit), but they could, and did, get fruit by asking for it.

At some distance in the rear of the white folks' house stood the barns and other outhouses, and a little to the east of these was the large horse and cow lot and the stables. In front was a beautiful avenue skirted on each side with lovely oaks of different varieties. And, strange to say, about three hundred yards in front of the white folks' house, and to the east of this beautiful avenue, was located the "negro quarters." On most plantations in those days the "negro quarters" was located in the rear, or at least some distance from the white folks' house. But not so in this case, for these were located in front, but a little distance from the house and from the avenue. But there is another thing that goes to show that the owners and managers of this plantation were people of education, culture and refinement, and that was even the fields were given names. At some distance eastward from the "big house" was a large field called "Sykes field." In the midst of this field stood a large and beautiful walnut tree. It was customary to plant wheat, oats or rye in this field, and when the crop was harvested, which usually took place in June, the field was then made a pasture. Every field of the plantation had a good fence around it, and after the crops were taken off the horses, cattle and sheep were turned in. It was a charming sight to see these creatures during the early morning grazing in different parts of the "Sykes field," and when the sun waxed hot they would gather themselves together and lie down under this tree and rest. And in the cool of the afternoon they would start out again. This was repeated day by day during the summer season. Still east of the "Sykes field," and across the swamp, were two large fields called the upper and lower "Forks." North of these was another called the "Island field." Then there were the "New Ground field," the "Gin House field," the "Middle field," the "Graveyard field" and the "West field." It was necessary that these fields should all have names so that it could be ascertained where the hands were working, or where the horses or cows were being pastured.

There were six horses and two mules on the place, and they, too, all had names. There was

"Old Reuben," "Old Gray," "Old Lep," "Fannie," "John" and "Charlie." John and Charlie were young horses raised on the place. The mules were "Jack" and "Ginnie." Jack was a noble fellow, but Ginnie was as wicked as she could be. She had as many devils in her as did Mary Magdalene before she met Christ. Ginnie did very well when hitched to the wagon with Jack or some other horse by her side, but under the saddle she would not carry double to save your life. And pull a plow, that depended on the state of her mind. If she felt like it she would do it, but if she did not she would kick things to pieces in a jiffy. When that mule was foaled she was as good as it is possible for a mule to be, but the negro who plowed her spoilt her. And if Ginnie had been granted the gift of speech as was the good fortuné of Balaam's ass, she doubtless would have said to that negro and to the rest of mankind in the language of Shakespeare: "Villainous company hath been the spoil of me."

It will be noticed that the word "old" precedes the names of these horses. This does not signify that they were naturally old, but it was simply a designation given to them by the slaves, and the white folks accepted it and so styled the horses also. The slaves were adepts at giving nicknames to animals, to each other and even to the white folks. But the white folks seldom caught on to the nicknames given to them.

I cannot close this chapter without speaking of the adjoining plantations. To the north was Mr. Isaac Keels and his father, Mr. Billie Keels; east was Mr. Alex. Lemons; south was Mr. Chris. Player, and west was Mr. Fullwood and Mr. Jack Player. The latter was a brother of Mr. Chris. Player. These all were slaveholders, but none of them were cruel to their slaves. They knew that the slaves were valuable property, and, therefore, took good care of them. Mr. Fullwood died, leaving a widow and a number of small children, and the estate could not be settled up until the youngest child became of age. This made it necessary to put the plantation in the hands of an overseer, and that overseer was Mr. Rance Player, a brother of Mr. Chris. Player and Jack Player. He was pretty strict in his discipline, but not cruel. Such things as bloodhounds and nigger traders were scarce in that community. I will not say that they were never seen, but they were scarce. It was a rare thing for slaves to be bought and sold in that neighborhood.

I quote a couple of verses from "Lyrics of Love," by Rev. Charles Roundtree Dinkins, a negro poet. The book was published by *The State Publishing Company of Columbia, S. C.*:

"Give me the farm, where grows the corn,
Shouting with tassel gold unworn,
While breezes roll;
Where smiles the fleecy staple, white,
Like snowy fields of Ėden bright
Around the soul.

"Give me the farm—the cabin dear,
With the fireplace so spacious there—
Full five feet wide—
With the backlog just burning down,
Potatoes sweet and 'possum brown
Right by my side."

CHAPTER II.

THE PROPRIETOR OF THE OLD PLANTATION.

The owner of this farm was a remarkable character. His name was Mr. John Frierson, but he was called by his intimate friends "Jack Frierson." There was another John Frierson, who lived in the upper part of Sumter County, but this one was sometimes alluded to as "John Frierson on Pudden Swamp," to distinguish him from the other Mr. John Frierson. His age I do not know, but he lived to be quite an old man.

He was a Christian and was, perhaps, the leading man in the Shiloh Methodist Church. I am told that he was educated for the Christian ministry in early life, but he never entered that holy calling. But he became a class leader, and this was the only sacred office he would accept, and he filled it well and to the satisfaction of the ministers and the members of the Shiloh Church. It was said that he was the best educated man in all that region of country. He was a very fine elocutionist and one of the best readers that ever opened a book or held a newspaper. During the exciting times that led up to the War Between the States, and during the four years of that bloody struggle, the white neighbors—and many of them were men and women of wealth and intelligence—used to come to the home of Mr. Frierson to hear him read the papers and to discuss with him the news and the burning questions of that day.

Mr. Frierson was married three times. By his first wife there was born but one child—a boy—whom he named Mack; by his second wife there were born five children—three girls and two boys, and by his last wife there was no issue. The children by his second wife were named as follows: Mary Ann, Isabella, Rush, Adolphus and Janie. I have given them in the order of their birth, as I remember it. These all grew up to manhood and womanhood. The following lived to be married off: Mack, Isabella, Adolphus and Janie.

Mr. Mack married a lady from Chesterfield County whose maiden name was Miss Martha Garland. Her father's name was Mr. Jesse Garland. He was a farmer, owned a few slaves, but his daughter—Miss Martha—was handsome and considered a belle in society. Miss Isabella married Mr. Ransom Garland, the brother of Miss Martha. Mr. Adolphus married the daughter of Mr. Billie Keels, known as "Little Billie Keels." Miss Janie married a Mr. Kirby and afterwards settled in Columbia, S. C., as I have been informed. I also learned that she has some sons, and possibly grandsons living there now, and are merchants in that city. Miss Mary Ann never married, but lived to be a very pious and happy old maid. She became housekeeper for her father after the death of her mother and until he married again, which was his third and last marriage. Her own mother was a very devout Christian, and spared no pains in training up her children in the way they should go, so that when they became old they did not depart from it.

Mr. Rush grew up to a beautiful young manhood and became quite a favorite among the young ladies of the community, but the war broke out and there was a call for volunteers, and he was among the first to enter the Confederate army. His leaving the old plantation to go to the front was a sad occasion. Well do I remember the morning. The handsome young soldier in a beautiful new uniform of gray with shining buttons bade the family and servants good-bye, never to return. In less than two years he fell on one of the battlefields of Virginia, and sacrificed his life for the cause that is so dear to every Southern white man. When the news of his death reached the old plantation there was mourning and weeping among the white folks and the slaves. He was a good young man, and was much beloved by all. His body was never brought home, but was buried in that far-off land along with his comrades in battle. But he was a Christian, having been brought up in a religious atmosphere, and by devout parents, and, on the other side of the mystic river, he has met them, where peace forever abides and where happiness is the lot of all such.

> "Asleep in Jesus! far from thee
> Thy kindred and their graves may be;
> But thine is still a blessed sleep,
> From which none ever wakes to weep."

Mr. Mack, the oldest son, was also a devout young man. Like Jacob of old, he was a man of prayer. There was a place in the thicket in the rear of the lot where he resorted for private communion with his Maker every evening at twilight. When the day's work was done, and when the horses and mules were stabled and fed, he would steal away to his sacred retreat and pour out his soul in prayer. Many were the times when the writer of these lines, then a boy of twelve, stood in the road just a short distance away from his place of prayer, when the stars were being revealed in the heavens and the crimson gradually fading away from the sunset skies, and listened alternately to the plaintive sounds of the whippoorwill and the audible voice of prayer, which was tremulous with emotion and frequently accompanied with tears. The scene was awe-inspiring to the inquiring mind and to the reverent soul, such as mine was at that time. I must confess that I scarcely knew what it all meant. But I sure did love to hear Mr. Mack pray and the whippoorwill hollo. But, thank God, I have lived long enough to know what prayer means.

But let us consider our subject a little further. Mr. Frierson invariably observed family worship twice a day—morning and evening. The Scriptures were read in course at each service. Singing was usually omitted except on special occasions, when perhaps there was a minister present, one who could sing. But he was never in such a hurry that he did not have time for family devotions. It mattered not in what season of the year and how busy they might be in the farm, his prayers he would say. And it was always a treat to hear that man read his Bible and then to take the different members of his family to a throne of grace. And his slaves were not forgotten during these warm, fervent and eloquent intercessary prayers.

Mr. Frierson always looked carefully after the morals of his slaves. I have already stated that he did not allow them to steal if he could possibly prevent it. He did everything he could to teach them to be truthful, to be honest, and to be morally upright. He had it understood on his plantation that there should be no little bastard slaves there. He gave it out that they were not wanted. When the boys and girls reached a marriageable age he advised them to marry, but marry some one on the plantation, and he would see to it that they should not be separated. But if they married some one from the adjoining plantations, they might be separated eventually by the "nigger traders," as they were called in that day and time. But Mr. Frierson was never known to separate a man and his wife by sale or by trading. Nor was he ever known to separate mother and child. He did not believe in this kind of business.

Mr. Frierson was a good man and taught both his children and servants to fear God and keep His commandments. The Lord said of Abraham, "For I know him that he will command his children and his household after him, and they shall keep the way of the Lord, to do justice and judgment." These words may fitly be applied to our subject—Mr. Frierson—for he certainly emulated the example of the Father of the faithful.

There were some free colored people in the neighborhood. Some of these were free-born, but others bought their freedom. But all of them, according to the then existing laws, had to have some white man to be their guardian.

That is, some white man to look after their interest to see that they got their rights, and to protect them, if necessary. And Mr. Frierson was chosen by some of these free colored people as their guardian. He was a kind-hearted man and never failed to respond to the call of distress. It mattered not whether it came from the poor slave or from the more fortunate freeman or from the oppressed white brother, he had an ear to hear the call, a heart to respond and hands to help. As Alfred Tennyson said of the Duke of Wellington, so I say of our subject: "The path of duty was the way to glory."

He seemed not to care what men thought of him, but his whole aim was to please his Maker. He regarded the voice of conscience as the voice of God, and to the warnings and mandates of that voice he was always true.

He was greatly beloved by all his neighbors. His children, his slaves and all his white associates loved and admired him. And when time shall be lost in the brilliant dawn of eternity's morning, many shall rise up and call him blessed.

"Asleep! asleep! when soft and low
The patient watchers come and go,
Their loving vigil keeping;
When from the dear eyes fades the light,
And the glad spirit takes its flight,
We speak of death as 'sleeping.'

"Or when, as dies the orb of day,
The aged Christian sinks away,
And the lone mourner weepeth;
When thus the pilgrim goes to rest,
With meek hands folded on his breast,
And his last sigh a prayer confessed—
We say of such, 'He sleepeth.'"

LUCY A. BENNETT.

CHAPTER III.

GRANNY, THE COOK, ON THE OLD PLANTATION.

The number that constituted the body of slaves on this plantation was not very large, but they were a fine-looking set of human beings. They were warmly clad, well fed and humanely treated. And, as forty-two years have passed since "the breaking up of the old plantation," it is hardly possible that the writer should remember the name of every slave born and raised on that place. And yet he can recall the most of them and the image of their person still yet lingers in his memory.

Here they are: There were Uncle Fridie and Aunt Nancy, his wife; Uncle Isom and Aunt Tena, his spouse. There were two young women on the plantation—Namie and Peggie—who, after marriage, became very fruitful. Namie married a man by the name of Tom and Peggie a man by the name of Sam. Tom belonged to a Mr. Durant, and Sam to a Mr. Singletary. Namie became the mother of some nine children and Peggie some twelve or thirteen. Namie's children were Melton, Sam, Nellie, Tom, Kellie, Jimmie, Vinie, Martha and Joe. Peggie's were Prince, Caroline, Sydney, Mary, Henry, Elizabeth, Aleck, Sammie and four or five others whose names I cannot now recall. Nearly all of these grew up to manhood and womanhood and marired off, and themselves became fathers and mothers. And when the Emancipation Proclamation was issued by Mr. Lincoln, there were perhaps forty or fifty slaves on this plantation.

But one of the most important characters among them all was Granny, the cook. She was slightly lame in one leg. When she was a little girl she and other children were playing in a bed of deep sand. She ran and jumped into the sand, and as her feet sunk into it she suddenly turned around and this twisted her leg at the knee. The injury at first did not seem to be serious and no doctor was called, but her leg grew crooked and she became lame for life. Because of this lameness she was favored to the extent that she was not made a field hand, but was kept about the house and taught to cook. And right well did she learn her trade; for she became one of the most expert cooks in all that region of country. And she took special pride in her profession, especially when company came to visit the white folks. All they had to do was to give Granny the materials and tell her what to do with them, and it was done. She always carefully followed the instructions given by Mrs. Frierson or Miss Mary Ann, and all was right. When that breakfast, that dinner or that supper was sent into the dining room, especially when company was "in the house," if the reader had been privileged to look upon it, or to sniff its delicious odor, he would have thought that there was a Parisian caterer who presided over that kitchen.

Mr. Frierson's house was the preacher's home. Like the Shunammite of old, he set apart a room in his house and denominated it the "prophet's chamber." He never forgot to entertain strangers, knowing that thereby some had entertained angels unawares. Among the preachers who served the Lynchburg circuit were: Rev. L. M. Little, Rev. M. A. Connolly, Rev. W. L. Pegues, Rev. W. W. Mood, Rev. P. F. Kistler, and Rev. F. Auld. These were all members of the South Carolina Conference of the M. E. Church, South. There were two eminent local preachers who preached acceptably to the people, namely: Rev. Jesse Smith and Rev. William Smith. These two ministers were brothers, and the latter, Rev. William Smith, was the father of three distinguished Carolinians, namely: the late Bishop A. Coke Smith, Rev. Charles B. Smith, and the Hon. E. D. Smith. But whenever these ministers would preach at the Shiloh church they would invariably come to Mr. Frierson's either for dinner or to pass the night. And when Granny, the cook, was notified that the pastor was coming, she would be delighted and made extensive preparations in the kitchen and did her best. All of Mr. Frierson's guests soon learned who the cook was, and seldom failed to give expressions of satisfaction when they left the dining room. Because of Granny's skill, Mr. Frierson did not have much trouble in persuading his pastors and friends to accept the hospitality of his home.

Granny could not be excelled in making and baking bread. Her biscuits, her light bread and her johnnie cakes were, to use a modern expression, "just out of sight." Reader, do you know what a "johnnie cake" is? I am afraid that you don't. If you have never inhaled the odor nor tasted a johnnie cake I am sure I shall have some difficulty in making you understand what it is. It was not baked in an oven nor in a stove, but before the fire.

A board was made out of oak, hickory or ash wood. It was about six inches wide and twelve inches long, and highly polished. The ingredients of the johnnie cake were: corn meal and sweet potatoes for flour, butter for lard and pure sweet milk for water. I think eggs were also used and some other seasoning, which I cannot now recall. These things were carefully mixed in and then the dough was spread out over the johnnie cake board and placed on the hearth before an oak fire. The board was slightly tilted so as to throw the cake squarely before the fire. It would soon "brown," as they said, and when Granny pronounced it done, the very sight, to say nothing of the odor, would make anybody's mouth water. Oh, how those preachers did like johnnie cake! Sometimes they would send for Granny to come into "the house" and shake her hand and congratulate this dusky queen of the kitchen.

It is said that women have a horror for snakes, and it is true. Ever since Mother Eve was beguiled by a serpent, all of her daughters—it matters not what their color may be, whether white, black or brown—have an awful dread of snakes. This intense hatred of the serpent tribe on the part of the women is of divine origin. In the Book it is written: "I will put enmity between thee and the woman and between thy seed and her seed; it shall bruise thy head and thou shalt bruise his heel." Thus spake the Lord to the serpent in the Garden of Eden.

But I want to tell the reader a story about Granny and the snake. The kitchen where Granny did the cooking was a small board building that set some distance from the dining room. It was about fifteen feet wide by twenty feet long. It had two doors—the doors being in the sides and opposite each other—and two windows. The building was unceiled. It was a mere shell. There was not even a loft overhead. This made it a den for rats, and, in consequence of this, a place for snakes. The rats came in search of food and the snakes came in search of rats.

One evening just about dark Granny was getting supper, and while stooping down at the fireplace a great big chicken snake was chasing a rat on the plate above. They turned the corner and while passing over the fireplace where Granny was stooping, the snake fell full length across her neck and instantly wrapped itself around her neck. It is needless to say that Granny alarmed the place. She hollered, she screamed; the dogs barked and the children cried. The white folks and the colored folks all came running to see what was the matter. Granny left the kitchen and took the yard, and the yard was a very large one, too. Doubtless the snake would have fled from fright, but Granny clutched it with both hands—one hand on each side of her neck. The men folks could not catch her to release her from the snake until she fainted, then they killed the snake and Granny soon came to. She was not bitten but greatly frightened. The white women had to finish getting the supper, while Granny tried to get herself together again, which she eventually succeeded in doing. But this was an experience which Granny never forgot. In subsequent years she used to sit down with a dozen or more children at her feet and relate to them, in graphic language, her experience with that old chicken snake. And oh, how the little ones used to ply her with questions! But she answered all of them to their satisfaction.

But Granny was great along other lines and for other things than that of cooking. It has already been stated that when Mr. Frierson lost his first wife she left a little motherless baby behind. It was a little boy, and his name was Mack. But Granny came to the child's rescue and acted a mother's part. She raised him. She prepared his food and fed him. She bathed him, dressed him, took him on her lap, tied his shoes, combed his hair and taught him his prayers. He slept in Granny's own bed with his lily white arms around her black neck. Little Mack loved Granny and Granny loved little Mack. And when he became a man he always entertained a high regard for her, and loved her to the end.

Granny, though she was black, considered herself the mistress on that plantation. She thought that her color was no fault of hers, but circumstances (part of the time Mr. Frierson having no wife) and efficiency, made her head of the household. When Granny gave orders those orders had to be obeyed. White and colored respected and obeyed her.

Granny took great delight in caring for the chickens and the turkeys. She also gave the pigs about the yard some attention. All the waste from the kitchen was carefully saved for them. She saw that the cows were milked regularly. She kept the milk piggins and pans clean and nice, and did the churning herself. Consequently Mr. Frierson always had a plenty of fatted fowls for his table and a pig to roast whenever he felt like it. He also had an abundance of nice milk and butter. Granny took special pride in providing these things, and her master felt grateful to her for it.

Granny lived to see Emancipation, and, after becoming free, was taken by her son-in-law to his own hired home, where she was tenderly cared for until the angels came and escorted her soul home to that "happy land far, far away." She lived the life of the righteous, and died in the Christian faith.

CHAPTER IV.

A 'Possum Hunt on the Old Plantation.

There was a good supply of fresh water fish in Pudden Swamp in ante-bellum days. The varieties known and caught in those days were suckers, pikes, jacks, perches and catfish. But the slaves hadn't much time for fishing; they had to work during the day. But they were very fond of hunting coons and 'possums, and even this pastime had to be gratified at night.

The flesh of these animals, when properly prepared, makes a very savory and palatable dish. The method of cooking the 'possum or coon was this: They first parboiled it whole and then roasted or baked it brown. Sweet potatoes were also boiled and skinned and roasted around it. The slaves were very fond of such dishes.

As has already been remarked, the young men had a natural fondness for hunting. Like the sporting men of all races, there were some slaves who possessed a natural fondness for the chase.

There were four dogs belonging to the white folks and perhaps one or two belonging to the slaves. These were all trained by the slaves. There was old Sumter, named for General Sumter of Revolutionary fame, and old Bull, Rip and

Tiz. The last two were full-blood fox hounds, male and female. Better 'possum and coon dogs never entered the woods. Then there was old Toler. He was half bull and belonged to Tom. He was the fighter. When the other dogs failed he would swing to a 'possum or coon to the last. A 'possum was not much at fighting, unless he was caught in his den, then it took all the dogs to bring him out, and often all failed but old Toler. He would bring him out or die. Consequently the boys seldom left him behind. His presence was necessary to do the fighting.

'Possums usually inhabit the woodland and coons the swamps. The boys thought that they would like to have a 'possum for their Sunday morning's breakfast, and yet they had been told by Uncle Fridie and Uncle Isom not to go hunting on Saturday night, for, as the holy Sabbath began at midnight and as they had no way of telling when midnight came, they would be likely to hunt on Sunday. They owned no watches, but were told that when the seven stars reached a point directly overhead that it was midnight. Such was the case at that season of the year.

After supper the boys started out. The only things necessary to achieve a successful hunt was the dogs and two or three good, sharp axes with which to cut down the trees when the dogs would tree the game. They first went to the woods for a 'possum hunt, but, after wandering away for two miles, the dogs failed to strike a trail. They then concluded to go to the swamp (Pudden Swamp), for a coon hunt. Away then went, holding in their hands bright pitch pine torches. Now and then they would give to the dogs a keen coon hunters' whoop, but there came no response from them. On they went in the dark and dense swamp, whooping up the dogs. Presently the clear, full yelp of old Bull was heard. Sydney said, "It is a rabbit, for old Bull likes to run rabbits." "Wait and see," said Tom. Sam, who was the oldest in the crowd, and who had more experience in the hunting business than all the others, said: "I am waiting on old Tiz, for she never runs rabbits at night. If she barks then I will know it's a coon." Again the boys whooped to the dogs. Just then a long, rolling bark was heard, such as a full-blood fox hound would make when it strikes a warm trail. Sam said: "Boys, it is old Tiz, and I believe it is a coon. Come on." The torch-bearers snuffed their torches and quickened their steps. Again the boys whooped. By this time all four of the dogs, as the hunters used to say, were speaking. Old Bull, old Sumter, Rip and Tiz. The sound of their barking and yelping was like different voices singing the four parts of music. There was the soprano, alto, tenor and bass. Again the boys whooped. On they went trying to keep up with the dogs. The fellows got lively as they thought of the fun just ahead of them, when they would have the pleasure of witnessing a great coon-dog fight. But all of a sudden every dog ceased barking and the hunters stopped. They did not know what to make of it. Again they whooped, but there was no response on the part of the dogs. They listened in silent wonder. Presently the dogs came in, one by one, with their tails drooping between their hind legs. The boys noticed that their bristles were all upturned and they whined at their feet. The hunters became frightened and they began to think. Tom said, "Boys, perhaps it is after midnight and we are hunting on Sunday." Instantly all eyes were upturned as they peered into the heavens looking for the seven stars, and to their surprise the seven stars had passed the zenith and swung far over into the western sky. Then they remembered what Uncle Fridie and Uncle Isom had told them about hunting on Sunday. Immediately they all concluded that God was angry with them for desecrating His holy day, and allowed the devil to come after them. It is needless to say that they left the swamp unceremoniously, for such was the case. They ran nearly every step of the way home, and when they got their breath they awoke the whole negro quarters and related their wonderful but very unpleasant experience. All the slaves believed that it was the devil sent after those wicked boys, but when the white folks heard of it they said it was a bear, for Mr. Adolphus saw one just a few days before while squirrel hunting in that region. But the slaves all held to their belief and still contended that it was the devil and that he came in the form of a big black bear. Suffice it to say that it cured the boys, and from that time on there was no more 'possum and coon hunting by the slaves on Saturday night in all that part of the country.

CHAPTER V.

A Wedding on the Old Plantation.

The slave young men and young women were like the young people of all other races, they fell in love and they married. Their love affairs, their courtship and their marriage were of the simplest form. They could not read nor write, therefore notes and letters did not figure in their love experiences. But they loved all the same. Cupid managed to kindle the divine spark in their breasts, and he had a way to fan it to a flame.

Love, as every one who has loved knows, has a language peculiarly its own. And it is not a language of words, but rather a language like that of free masonry. It is a language of grips, of signs and of symbols. When two young slaves fell in love with each other the young man would make it known on his part by a gentle pressure of the young woman's hand as they shook hands. Or he would give her a peculiar or affectionate smile and accompany his action with a loving gift. And in the majority of cases the gift consisted in the most beautiful red apple that he could secure from the orchard. The girl would rarely eat the apple until the Sabbath was passed and until it had become mellow. The presentation would likely be made on the Sabbath as they went or returned from church, and the girl invariably carried the apple in her hand or wrapped it in her handkerchief. As she gazed upon its beauty and inhaled its fragrance, she would be reminded of the tender love of her sweetheart.

When the young man became satisfied that he had won the heart of his girl, he then proceeded gently and modestly to ask her to become his wife. This was called among the slaves "popping the question." Having secured her consent, he next secured the consent of her parents, if she had any, and the consent of his master and her master, if she lived on another plantation. This ended it. He was considered married, and he took her to be his wife. This was the usual way. There was no religious wedding ceremony and no marriage supper.

But there were a few isolated cases where the slaves were allowed to marry in due form and were given a wedding supper. These were the more prominent or favorite slaves, such as butlers, coachmen, nurses, chambermaids or cooks, sometimes enjoyed this privilege. Sam, the foreman on Mr. Frierson's plantation, was granted such a favor. He married a girl whose name was Bettie. She belonged to Mr. Isaac Keels, who owned the adjoining plantation just north of Mr. Frierson's.

The time was Saturday night and the occasion was a great one. Careful and elaborate preparations were made. The Friersons on Sam's side, and the Keelses on Bettie's side, co-operated to make the wedding a success. Also the relatives of the bride and the groom came forward to render assistance.

There were six bridesmaids and six groomsmen. The bridesmaids were all dressed in white and the groomsmen in black. Most of these costumes were borrowed—some from the white folks and some from the colored. The marriage feast was a bountiful affair. A good size shote, the gift of Mr. Frierson, was nicely barbecued. Uncle Tom, the father of the groom, was an expert at barbecuing. He did a lot of it for the white folks, especially on occasions of general musters, weddings, picnics, etc. Dozens of chickens were roasted, potted and fried. An abundance of sweet potato custards, apple pies and cakes were baked, and several large pots of rice were boiled. Every plantation within a radius of five miles was represented at that wedding. The marriage took place at the bride's home, or, I might say, in the negro quarters on Mr. Isaac Keels' place. Several white folks were present, especially of the Friersons and the Keelses. Uncle John

Woods, an ante-bellum negro preacher, was engaged to perform the marriage ceremony. He was a very intelligent old man. He could read well and talk fluently. He was considered a great preacher by the slaves, and many of the devout white folks were fond of hearing him. He wore black pants and a black shad-belly or pigeon-tail coat and white vest. It was a second-hand outfit, and was the gift of his old master, Mr. Woods. He also wore a black silk beaver hat that looked rather seedy because of its extreme age and exposure to the elements. He wore a stiff standing white collar that spanned his neck and touched his ear on each side, and a white tie. But, withal, he had the appearance of a distinguished negro clergyman of ante-bellum days.

The marriage ceremony took place in the yard. At some distance in front of the door of the two-room cabin was placed a small table with a clean white cloth over it and on which were two brass candlesticks. In these burned two tallow dips or candles. Behind this table stood the preacher. Near him sat Jerry Goodman in a chair with a fiddle, who played the wedding march. The waiters, as they were called, filed out in couples, a man and a woman walking together. The groom and his bride followed in the rear, with the bride gracefully leaning upon the arm of her beloved.

As now, so then, everybody tried to gain a view of the pair. Perfect silence reigned while Uncle John read, in a full, clear voice, the Methodist marriage ceremony. At the end the preacher was the first to kiss the bride, the groom the second, then followed kisses from all the bridesmaids and groomsmen. This was the custom in ante-bellum days among the slaves.

The next thing in order was the supper. Two tables had been built on different sides of the yard, one for the white folks and the other for the colored. The table for the white folks was about twelve feet long and three feet wide; the one for the colored was about twenty feet long and three wide. Clean white cloths were spread over these tables and plates were placed thereon as close as persons could stand. Food was put upon these tables until, if they were things of life, they would literally have groaned under the burdens of good things. Uncle John was placed at the head of the colored people's table with the groom and his bride on the right and the groomsmen and bridesmaids on each side down the line. He asked the divine blessing, or said the grace, for both tables. There were several tables full of the guests, but, as the food supply was ample, all had enough. The whole scene was a picturesque one, and it was made more so by the glare of the big bonfire that was kept burning in the yard.

After supper the fiddle struck up, with the nimble fingers of Jerry Goodman on the bow, and the dancing began and continued until a very late hour of the night. Early in the next week Sam, the groom, settled the marriage fee by giving the preacher, Uncle John Woods, a peck of clean-beat rice. Thus ended the wedding festivities on the old plantation.

CHAPTER VI.

Christmas on the Old Plantation.

Not many of the slaves knew the historical significance of Christmas. They could not read nor write, hence their knowledge of the important events of history, even those of sacred history, was exceedingly limited. Most they knew about Christmas was that it meant a good time for everybody. It was the custom on the plantations in that region of the country to kill the fattening hogs just before Christmas so that all, white folks and slaves, might have plenty of fresh meat to eat during this joyous season. This gave rise to the expression, which originated among the slaves, "a hog-killing time." Backbones, spare-ribs and rice were a favorite dish about Christmas time.

There is another thing to be considered about the way and manner in which Christmas was observed on the old plantation in ante-bellum days, and that is this: Three days were usually given to the slaves for Christmas. The day before, generally called "Christmas Eve," and the day after; hence the slaves thought all three days were Christmas. They frequently referred to Christmas Eve as "the first day of Christmas," to Christmas itself as "the second day of Christmas," and the day after as "the third or last day of Christmas." And this thought and this manner of expression have been brought over into freedom. Among the country colored people we frequently hear similar expressions used even at this day and time in speaking of Christmas.

On some plantations it was the custom to have all the slaves repair in a body to the white folks' house on Christmas morning and receive a dram as "a Christmas present." Old and young, male and female, came forward for the "Christmas dram." It was certainly a lively time with the slaves on the old plantation. Those who came early to the yard would have to wait until all came. And while they waited they would whistle, jig or dance, or

"They sat and sung
Their slender ditties when the trees were bare."

But this was not the case on Mr. Frierson's plantation. He was a Christian man, and, therefore, believed in and practiced the principles of temperance. He, nor a single member of his family, were ever known to indulge in strong drink. Such a thing as whiskey was unknown on that plantation. But it was freely used on some of the adjoining plantations. On some of these there were drunkards to be found both among the white folks and among the slaves. But not so on Mr. Frierson's place. It was a plantation where sobriety was strictly taught and practiced by the white folks, and, consequently, the slaves were greatly benefited.

But Christmas was observed on Mr. Frierson's place in a way that was highly enjoyable to all. It was the custom on all the plantations around to give at the beginning of the winter each male among the slaves a new outfit, consisting of shoes, pants, coat and a cap. The women and girls got shoes and dresses. Mr. Frierson made it a point to give out these on Christmas morning.

On or about a month before Christmas the right foot of each slave, male and female, was measured and Mr. Frierson would get in his buggy and drive to Sumter, the County seat, and Sam would bring the two-horse wagon. The purpose was to buy shoes for the slaves. The town was only about twenty miles away, and by starting before day they could, and did, make the trip in a day, and do all their trading, too. The topic of conservation during that day among the slaves while they worked was the trip of the old boss and Sam to Sumter. As the sun went down and the time drew near for them to return the slaves would listen for the rumbling of the wagon wheels and the sound of horses' hoofs. That night their slumbers were filled with dreams and visions of new suits, new shoes, new caps and new dresses. But these things were not given out until Christmas morning. And while this glad day was perhaps only a month off, yet the month seemed longer, the days seemed longer and the nights seemed longer than at any other season of the year. This was naturally and literally true of the nights, but it was not true of the days nor the month, but so it seemed to the slaves. The anxiety, the longing and the solicitude for the dawn of Christmas morning is indescribable. The thought of old Santa Claus among enlightened people never could produce such a feeling as that which animated the breasts of these poor, ignorant slaves.

But Christmas came. The sun arose without a cloud to obscure his brightness. Breakfast is over and all hands repair to the "house." Presently the yard is full of darkies with smiling faces and joyous hearts. And there are as many piles on that long front piazza of the white folks' house as there are hands on that place. In each pile there are shoes, a suit, or dress, and a cap. On each pile there is a tag with the name of the person written on it for whom it is designed. Now, imagine, if you can, the exquisite joy that thrilled each heart as his or her name was called.

And as each person filed out of that gate on their return to the negro quarters they seemed to be as happy as angels. And it is needless to say that the white folks enjoyed the distribution of the winter's outfit on Christmas morning as much as the slaves, for such undoubtedly was the case. Everybody felt that this was a better way than having a dram on Christmas morning. Such was Christmas on the old plantation in ante-bellum days.

CHAPTER VII.

SUNDAY ON THE OLD PLANTATION.

Sunday was always a welcome day on the old plantation, not only by the slaves, but also by the white folks. It came in all right to break the monotony of plantation life. The older and more serious ones went to "meetin'" or visited the sick, or made social calls, while the youngsters met other youngsters from the adjoining plantations and spent the day in wrestling, jumping, boxing, running foot races and sometimes fighting. In the summer season they would sometimes roam through the fields from plantation to plantation in search of watermelons and fruits. They would plunge into the dark and dense swamp in search of wild muscadine grapes or through the fields for blackberries, or the pine woods for huckleberries.

On some of the nearby plantations the younger slaves were made to do light work on Sunday, such as minding the birds and crows from the corn, rice and potatoes. When these plants were coming up the crows and rice birds were very destructive. They would pull them up, and often the whole crop would have to be carefully replanted. But Mr. Frierson, who planted the same kinds of stuff as was planted on the other plantations, did not put any of his slaves on guard in the fields on Sunday, and yet he always made good crops and had an abundance. He was a God-fearing man, and held that the Sabbath was a day of rest for man and beast. He kept the day as sacred and required all his slaves, as nearly as possible, to do the same.

The Shiloh Methodist Church, to which Mr. Frierson and his family belonged, formed a part of the circuit known as the "Lynchburg Circuit." The parsonage was located at Lynchburg, a little cross-roads village about eight miles away. The minister was accustomed to preach in the Methodist Church at Lynchburg Sunday morning at 11 o'clock and at Shiloh in the afternoon at 3:30 o'clock the same day. His appointment at the Shiloh Church was once a month, but to keep the slaves—and especially the younger ones—out of mischief, Mr. Frierson had preaching in his yard under the stately old water oaks on the regular preaching day at Shiloh. This service was conducted by some one of the old ante-bellum negro preachers. There was also a Sunday school conducted at the Shiloh Church in the afternoon just before preaching. All this was done for the spiritual and moral uplift of the slaves as well as to keep them out of devilment, and from desecrating God's holy day.

But the service conducted in Mr. Frierson's yard at 11 o'clock on the preaching day at Shiloh was the centre of attraction in all that region of country. The more pious from the adjacent plantations, both white and colored, came in large numbers. The services invariably were conducted by ante-bellum negro preachers. These preachers were: Uncle John Woods, Uncle Daniel Gass, Uncle Daniel Hand, and Uncle Joseph White. Some of these lived just a few miles away, others again lived a considerable distance. One, Uncle Daniel Hand, lived across the Lynches River, over in Darlington, the adjoining county. They all had their day, and they seldom failed to meet it. Of course, they had to get the consent of their masters to come, and they invariably brought a ticket from their masters for their protection. If they lived far away their masters would let them have a mule to ride; or if it happened to be in the work season and the mules were busy, the master's saddle horse or buggy horse was given instead. But Uncle John Woods lived the nearest, and, therefore, was oftenest there.

Mr. Frierson's front yard was a large one, and, as has been stated heretofore several times, it was well shaded with large and beautiful water oaks. Under these oaks Mr. Frierson had very comfortable seats placed. There was a seating capacity for possibly 250 or 300 people. They were arranged so that the audience would face the east and present a side view to the white folks, who sat in the long front piazza. At the east end of these seats, fronting the audience, stood a small table with a clean white cloth thrown over it. On this table was placed a pitcher of fresh water and a tumbler, a Bible and a hymn book, and behind it a chair. All this for the use and convenience of the speaker, who was always a colored man. No white preacher was ever known to stand behind that table, though some of them very much desired to do so. That long piazza was usually filled with devout white worshippers, and the seats below with zealous and enthusiastic colored Christians.

The scene presented a very unique appearance. Those who had religion in that day and time had what is now called "the old time religion." Sometimes when the old preacher would warm up to his subject and grow loud, if not eloquent, the audience would break forth in shouts of joy and praise. While some colored sister would be jumping out in the audience, some of the white ladies were known to act in a similar manner in the piazza. In those days both the white folks and the colored folks had good religion. The singing by the colored folks on such occasions was an important feature of the worship. It was not done by notes nor always by words, but it was from the heart, and the melody seldom failed to stir the soul. Rev. Dinkins, the negro poet quoted previously, describes it thus:

"Give me the farm when Sunday comes,
When all the girls and all the chums
Meet at the spring,
When long-eared mules, ox-carts in droves,
Come sailing through the woods and groves,
Oh, how we sing!

"The preacher reads the hymn divine,
And we remember not a line,
But sing right on;
When with the text we start to shout,
Forgetting shame, or pride, or doubt,
To heaven most gone."

Uncle John Woods was a good preacher, considering his chances, and had an excellent command of good English. He was a man of deep piety, and had the love and respect of both white and colored. The author herewith reproduces, from memory, one of his sermons preached in Mr. Frierson's yard.

A Sermon on the Old Plantation.

By Uncle John Woods.

Text—"The men of Nineveh shall rise in judgment with this generation and shall condemn it because they repented at the preaching of Jonas; and, behold, a greater than Jonas is here."—Matt. xii:41.

Brothers and Sisters: These words, which I have taken for a text, were spoken by our Lord, Jesus Christ. He spoke them to the people of His day and time, but He commanded His servant, St. Matthew, to write them down in a book so that all the people in all the ages might have them and take warning. So I bring them to you today, and you will do well to listen and to take heed.

St. Matthew was a servant, brothers and sisters, and he was a good servant and obeyed Christ, his Master. Christ called him and he came and followed Christ. Christ commanded him to write the gospel and he wrote it. So Christ wants you and me to obey Him in all things. He says, "Repent, for the kingdom of heaven is at hand." Christ wants us to hear His voice and obey His words. And if we don't obey Him he will punish us, for He says in another place: "He that knows his Master's will and does it not shall be beaten with many stripes." Many of us know, in a two-fold sense, what this means. But all who are not Christians will learn to their sorrow one of these days what it means in a spiritual sense. Christ is our Master, we are His servants, and if we don't obey Him and repent, He will certainly apply the lash, and apply it severely, too.

But let us consider Jonah. He is the man referred to in the text. Let me read it again; perhaps you have forgotten it: "The men of Ninevah shall rise in judgment with this generation and shall condemn it, because they repented at the preaching of Jonah; and, behold, a greater than Jonah is here."

Jonah was called just like Matthew. Matthew was called to be an apostle and to write a book, and he obeyed. Jonah was called to be a prophet. He was sent to preach repentance to the people of Ninevah, but he refused to go. It is hard to tell, brothers and sisters, what were his reasons for not obeying God and going to preach to these people. But I remember that Jonah was a Jew, and, according to his raising and training, he did not want to have anything to do with the people of another nation. He did not wish to associate with them, he did not wish to eat with them, nor sleep in their houses, nor to preach the word of God to them. I can't say Jonah was a wicked man, neither can I say he was a bad man, for I don't believe that God would call a wicked or a bad man to preach His word to the people, no, not even to the heathen.

Now, what did Jonah do? Let us see. He ran away, or, at least, he tried to run away from

God. He thought he would go down to Joppa, buy a ticket for Tarshish and take shipping for that place, as though there was no God in Joppa, Tarshish or on the sea. My friends, I fear we sometimes make the same mistake. We do wrong and then try to run away from God. We try to hide from His presence. Adam and Eve, in the Garden of Eden, tried the same trick, but it would not work. They sinned against God. They disobeyed Him and ate the forbidden fruit, and when they found that God was displeased and angry with them, they hid themselves among the bushes of the garden. But God came down and sought them and found them. Right there in the garden the judgment was set; the guilty pair was convicted and the awful sentence was pronounced. In great shame and disgrace they were driven from that holy place out into a world of sin, sorrow and misery. If a man breaks God's holy law and sin against Him, though he may run away and hide, God will find him and punish him. The Bible says, "Be sure your sins will find you out."

But Jonah came to Joppa, and, after paying his fare, he went aboard that ship. He did not feel good. He did not feel like a man taking a pleasure trip, nor like a man going off on business. He did not sit down on deck and converse with the other passengers. No, under the burden of his terrible guilt he went down into the hold of the ship among the freight and went fast to sleep. He went to sleep! Sleep is all right when it is taken in the right place, at the right time and under the right circumstances. Otherwise it is wrong, it is out of place. Hence you see, brothers and sisters, it is possible for a man to sleep with a great burden of guilt upon him, and when he is in great and fearful danger. Jonah was asleep, but God was wide awake with His eyes on him. Jonah thought he was hiding, but God saw him.

By and by I hear loud thunders begin to roll. I see dark clouds coming up. The lightnings flash and play upon the bosom of these black clouds. The sea roars and the waves rise like mountains. The ship pitches and rocks and the shipmaster and his crew become afraid. They threw some of the freight overboard and every man prayed to his god, and yet the storm was not abated. It still raged. Then they thought that they would cast lots to see on whose account this terrible storm had come upon them. They felt that somebody was guilty and they desired to find the guilty man. And when the lot was cast it fell upon Jonah. He was the guilty man. Then the shipmaster went down in the hold and found Jonah fast asleep. How that man could sleep in the midst of such a storm is a mystery to me! I cannot understand it. But every sinner is doing the same thing. He is dead asleep in his sins while the storm of God's wrath is raging all around him.

The shipmaster said to Jonah: "What meanest thou, O sleeper? arise, call upon thy God, if so be that God will think upon us, that we perish not." When Jonah was awakened, the shipmaster, his crew and the passengers all gathered around him and asked him what was his occupation, what was his country and what was his nation. And Jonah answered and said: "I am a Hebrew and I fear Jehovah, the God of heaven, who hath made the sea and the dry land." He then confessed his guilt. He told them that he was trying to run away from God, and begged them to throw him into the sea. They did so. But God had sent a great fish to swallow up Jonah. And Jonah was three days and nights in the belly of the fish. Then God told the fish to cast Jonah out on land, and the fish did so. And when Jonah got free from the fish he went to Nineveh and preached repentance to the people, and the whole city was converted and spared. Now, Jesus says in my text: "The men of Nineveh shall rise in judgment with this generation and shall condemn it, because they repented at the preaching of Jonah; and, behold, a greater than Jonah is here."

Christ declares here in this text that He is greater than Jonah. And so He is. This does not need any argument to prove it. You all believe that. Christ is greater than Jonah. Jonah was a man, Christ was God. Jonah was guilty of the sins of disobedience and anger, Christ yielded perfect obedience to God and was without sin. Therefore He is greater than Jonah. But the people of Ninevah repented at the preaching of Jonah, while Christ, who is greater than Jonah, came from heaven to earth to preach to sinners, and they will not hear nor repent. Therefore the people of Nineveh shall rise up in the judgment and condemn them.

My friends, there is going to be a judgment. God has appointed a day when He is going to judge the world. All the good angels will be there. All the devils in hell and out of hell will be there. All the good people saved in heaven will be there, and all the bad people lost in hell will be there. And you, my friends, all will be there, and I will be there. And if you don't repent the men of Nineveh will come forth as witnesses against you. They shall condemn you, because they repented at the preaching of Jonah, and behold a greater than Jonah is here, and that greater one is Christ.

May the Lord help you all to get ready for that awful day, for it will surely come!

This sermon, of which the above sketch is a mere outline, was delivered with great energy and power, and it produced a deep impression upon the entire audience.

CHAPTER VIII.

A Funeral on the Old Plantation.

It may appear strange to the reader, but it is true, nevertheless, that in some way or other the slaves very often connected sickness and death with voodooism or conjuration. This belief and practice of voodooism and conjuration originated in Africa, and was brought over to America when the native African was brought here and made a slave. The idea is deeply rooted in the negro thought and life. Its history runs back, perhaps, four thousand years among the native tribes of that Dark Continent.

I quote from the *University Encyclopedia:* "Voodoo, a name given by the negroes of the West Indies and the United States to superstitious rites and beliefs brought with them from Africa, and to the sorcerer who practiced these rites.

"In the Southern States of the Union there was at one time a widespread and deep-rooted belief in the power of these sorcerers. As the negroes advance in education the belief is dying away. At one time, however, despite all efforts of religious teachers to banish the mastery of this belief from the minds of the slaves, the voodoo "doctor' was an almost omnipotent individual in the estimation of his fellows. No slave could, under any pretext, be persuaded to expose himself to the vengeance or wrath of one of these conjurers. In some cases there was a reasonable foundation for these fears, for in not a few instances has it been proven that some of the voodoos were skillful poisoners, and while the great mass of their professed art was a rank imposture, still they possessed enough of devilish skill to render them objects of wholesome dread.

"Their methods were as varied and variable as the winds. Anything that was mysterious or likely to impress the ignorant mind with a feeling of terror was eagerly seized on and improved by them to their own advantage. Their services were more often invoked in destructive than in curative offices. If a negro desired to destroy an enemy he sought the aid of the voodoo, who, in many cases, would undertake to remove the obnoxious one, and the removal was generally accomplished through the medium of poison. No doubt exists that in many cases the victim of a voodoo died from sheer fright, for whenever a negro had reason to think that he was possessed by the spell of the voodoo, he at once gave up all hope, thus hastening the accomplishment of the end toward which the energies of the sorcerer were directed. Their incantations and spell-workings were always conducted with the greatest secrecy, no one being allowed to witness the more occult and potent portion of their ritual. They were frequently employed by dusky swains to gain for them the affections of their hard-hearted inamoratas, and love powders and other accessories for 'tricking' constituted their stock in trade, and in some instances yielded them no insignificant revenue. The field in which voodooism flourished best was the far South, among the rice, cotton and sugar plantations, where the negroes were not brought into contact so closely with their masters as they were further North."

The above quotation is a correct presentation of the conditions as they existed on the Frierson plantation, as well as on every plantation in the Southern States. What was true of one as regards voodooism and conjuration, was true of all of them.

Well, there was a girl on the Frierson plantation by the name of Mary. She was a black girl of medium size, but rather good looking. She was quite a favorite among the young men of the place and neighborhood. Several, so to speak, were cutting after her. Mary was a daughter of Aunt Peggie and Uncle Sam. But it came to pass that she took sick, and, after a lingering illness of possibly four or six months' duration, she died, leaving behind her a little infant. During the entire period of her sickness it was whispered around on the plantation, also on the adjoining plantations, that Mary had been conjured. Of course, this meant that she had been poisoned. There was a woman who lived on a plantation not far away, whose name was Epsey. This woman was said to have been Mary's rival in a love scrape, and, therefore, was accused of being the one who administered the dose. Some conjurer of the neighborhood prepared the dose for her, so it was said. This thing—Mary's sickness and death, and the talk of her being conjured—stirred the negroes on all the plantations for miles around.

But the white folks took no stock in all these rumors and gossip. They knew that Mary was sick, therefore they sent for Dr. Adolphus Higgins Frierson. He was a brother of the proprietor of the old plantation, and was a graduate of a medical college in Philadelphia, Pa. He was a learned man and a very competent physician. He was the family physician for the white folks, and also attended the slaves.

Dr. Frierson treated Mary, but the slaves did not think that he understood the case. Therefore they employed a voodoo doctor. This voodoo doctor said he understood the case perfectly well. He said Mary had been "hurt" or "conjured," and that he alone could cure her. So he treated her secretly at the same time that Dr. Frierson was treating her. But it came to pass that Mary died and her funeral was the largest ever held in all that region of the country.

Death always made a very profound impression upon the slaves. They could not understand it. Their dead was invariably buried at night or on the Sabbath, at which time the slaves from the adjoining plantations attended in large numbers. Mary's funeral took place at night.

The coffin, a rough home-made affair, was placed upon a cart, which was drawn by old Gray, and the multitude formed in a line in the rear, marching two deep. The procession was something like a quarter of a mile long. Perhaps every fifteenth person down the line carried an uplifted torch. As the procession moved slowly toward "the lonesome graveyard" down by the side of the swamp, they sung the well-known hymn of Dr. Isaac Watts:

> "When I can read my title clear
> To mansions in the skies,
> I bid farewell to every fear
> And wipe my weeping eyes."

Mary's baby was taken to the graveyard by its grandmother, and before the corpse was deposited in the earth, the baby was passed from one person to another across the coffin. The slaves believed that if this was not done it would be impossible to raise the infant. The mother's spirit would come back for her baby and take it to herself. This belief is held by many of the descendants of these slaves, who practice the same thing at the present day.

After this performance the corpse was lowered into the grave and covered, each person throwing a handful of dirt into the grave as a last and farewell act of kindness to the dead, and while this was being done the leader announced that other hymn of Dr. Watts:

"Hark! from the tombs a doleful sound
My ears, attend the cry;
Ye living men, come view the ground
Where you must shortly lie."

These hymns were sung with a spirit and pathos which were sufficient to move the heart of a savage. A prayer was offered, the doxology sung and the benediction was pronounced. This concluded the services at the grave. No burial or committal service was read, for it was only now and then that one could be found among the slaves who could read well enough to do it. At a subsequent time, when all the relatives and friends could be brought together, a big funeral sermon was preached by some one of the antebellum negro preachers. And this practice has been brought over into the land of freedom, and is still observed in some places and by some colored people at the present day.

CHAPTER IX.

A Log-Rolling on the Old Plantation.

The slaveholders of ante-bellum days had some customs that were very convenient, and, at the same time, very helpful to each other. There were no markets and butchers in the country, where they could get fresh meats: hence they formed a market among themselves, and each man was his own butcher. That is, a number of them formed themselves into a club, one of which killed a fat young beef every Saturday, and a choice piece was taken to each member of the club. Thus they were supplied with nice fresh beef every week. This beef was not sold, but was distributed around among the members of the club as a sort of an exchange arrangement. When a member of the club killed, he put the whole beef into the wagon (except his own choice or piece) and sent it round to each member of the club, and they made their own selection. When the club was formed, each member subscribed to, or promised to take so many pounds each week, and it was done. This arrangement obtained all through the country, and it worked very nicely.

There was another arrangement, which was formed by the planters for mutual helpfulness:

namely, the log-rolling. A day was set on which the log-rolling was to take place, and then invitations were sent out to the neighboring planters, and each sent a hand. This work was returned when the others had their log-rolling. A log-rolling always meant a good dinner of the best, and lots of fun, as well as a testing of manhood. This testing of manhood was something that everybody was interested in. The masters were concerned, and consequently they selected and sent to the log-rolling their ablest-bodied men; the slave women were concerned: for they wanted their husbands and sweethearts to be considered the best men of the community. Then, too, the men took great pride in the development of their muscles. They took delight in rolling up their shirt sleeves, and displaying the largeness of their arms. In some cases, their muscles presented the appearance of John L. Sullivan—the American pugilist.

The woodlands of the South were covered with a variety of trees and undergrowth. Among the trees, were to be found the majestic pine, the sturdy oak, the sweet maple, the lovely dogwood, and the fruitful and useful hickory. When a piece of woodland was cleared up, and made ready for planting, it was called "new ground." In clearing up new ground, the undergrowth was grubbed up and burned; the oaks, maples, dogwood, and hickories were cut down, split up, and hauled to the house for firewood; and the pines were belted or cut round, and left to die. After these pines had died and partially decayed, the winter's storms, from year to year, would blow them down: hence the necessity for the annual log-rolling. These log-rollings usually took place in the spring of the year. They formed an important part of the preparations for the new crop.

On the appointed day, the hands came together at the yard, and all necessary arrangements were made, the most important of which was the pairing or matching of the men for the day's work. In doing this, regard was had to the height and weight of the men. They were to lift in pairs, therefore, it was necessary that they should be as nearly the same height and weight as possible. The logs have all been cut about twenty feet in length, and several good, strong hand sticks have been made. Now, everything is ready, and away to the fields they go. See them as they put six hand-sticks under a great big log. This means twelve men—one at each end of the hand-stick. It is going to be a mighty testing of manhood. Every man is ordered to his place. The captain gives the order, "Ready," and every man bows to his burden, with one hand on the end of the hand-stick, and the other on the log to keep it from rolling. The next command given by the captain is, "Altogether!" and up comes the big log. As they walk and stagger toward the heap, they utter a whoop like what is known as the "Rebel yell." If one fails to lift his part, he is said to have been "pulled down," and therefore becomes the butt of ridicule for the balance of the day. When the women folks learn of his misfortune, they forever scorn him as a weakling.

At 12 o'clock the horn blows for dinner, and they all knock off, and go, and enjoy a good dinner. After a rest, for possibly two hours, they go to the field again, and finish up the work for the day. Such was the log-rolling in the "days before the war."

At a subsequent day the women and children gather up the bark and limbs of these fallen trees and throw or pile them on these log heaps and burn them. When fifty or seventy-five log heaps would be fully ablaze in the deepening of the evening twilight, the glare reflected from the heavens made it appear that the world was on fire. To even the benighted and uneducated slave, the sight was magnificent, and one of awe-inspiring beauty.

The custom of log-rolling, under the changed condition of things, may be done away with, but its name still lingers in the thought and language of modern times. It is often heard in gatherings, both religious and political, where everything goes, or is *made* to go *one way*. Such they say is "log-rolling." The idea comes from the fact that in a log-rolling, every man does his part, and every man goes the same way. There is unity of purpose, and concert of action. *This* is "log-rolling" in modern times.

CHAPTER X.

A Corn-Shucking on the Old Plantation.

All who have the good fortune to have been born and reared in the country, can recall with pleasing recollections the joy that welled up in all hearts during the harvest. Rev. Dr. Henry Duncan, an English writer of singular ability, says: "The heart thus opened, is prepared for that social enjoyment which we observe so remarkably diffused over whole bands of reapers engaged in the same toilsome but healthful employment. The emotion spreads from heart to heart, and the animation which prevails while the work proceeds, is not less an indication of gladness than the joke and song with which the welkin resounds during the intervals of rest. Who can view the joy which sparkles in the eye, and bursts from the lips of the reaper while he plies his daily tasks and not acknowledge a beneficent Creator?"

In the Book of Ruth we have a vivid and beautiful picture given us of an oriental harvest. The fields of Boaz teem with plenty. The golden crop yields its stores to replenish his granaries. The voice of the season calls for the reapers. They take down their sickles and whet them until they are keen and bright. Then away to the harvest-field they go, followed by the binders and gleaners; among the latter is the lovely Ruth. With patient industry they ply the sickle from morn till noon, at which time they gather, master, reapers, binders and gleaners, to partake of their bountiful meal. This they do with a beautiful simplicity and with great joy and gladness. And this joy and gladness is not the result of having a plenty to eat and drink, but the responsive gratitude of the finer qualities of the heart for the gracious and lavish gifts of a Divine Providence. This sentiment—joy at the return of the harvest—is characteristic of human nature. This is the testimony of all ages the world over. So it was with the ancient Egyptians, Greeks, and Romans. And so it is with us at the present day. The writer of these pages can remember the time when, even in America, the grain harvest was a time of great rejoicing. Of course this was before reapers or harvesters became so common. The neighbors for miles around used to send each a hand, with the old-fashioned "cradle," to our house, to assist in reaping down the harvest. And when ours was all done, we sent to help each of them. This was the custom in those days. With twenty hands we could reap down nearly a hundred acres in a day. Each reaper had a binder to follow him, and each binder had a little boy to gather up the handfuls as fast as the reaper would let them fall, and hand them to him or her. The writer was one of those little boys. It was fun for us. We always had a plenty to eat and drink of the best the farm afforded. The fun, the sport, and the joy we all had cannot be described. Only those who have had some acquaintance with farm life can imagine how we enjoyed it. What we ate and drank, and the joy the harvest afforded, constituted a considerable portion of our reward for bearing the burden and the heat of the day in the harvest field. This was wheat harvest, which usually occurred in June.

But the corn harvest came in the fall, and the corn-shucking always took place at that season. The fodder was generally pulled or stripped in August and September, and the ears of corn were left on the stock to dry until about the first of November. But now the day has come, and the corn breaking has begun. The hands all go to the field, and they break off the ears and throw them into piles. These piles are made in the middle of the same row about twenty feet apart, and contain the corn of some twelve rows. Two wagons, each drawn by a pair of mules or horses, with bodies the same size, are loaded level full of corn. At the barn yard it is thrown into two piles preparatory to the corn-shucking. One load is put on this pile, and the other on that, and so on, until the entire crop is hauled in.

Then the night is set for the corn-shucking: for it was usually had at night, so that the slaves from the adjacent plantations could come and enjoy the sport. Invitations were sent far and near, and they were readily accepted. Great preparations were made in food and drink. The only drink allowed at the corn-shucking was coffee, but it was customary on some of the plantations to have whiskey at corn-shuckings, but Mr. Frierson never allowed it.

It was often the case that from fifty to seventy-five men, beside the women, came to the corn-shucking. All these had to be fed. Great pots of rice, meat, bread and coffee were prepared. It was enough for all who came and took part in the corn-shucking.

When all the invited hands had arrived, the first thing in order was the election of two men to be captains, and these captains selected their companies from the crowd present. It was done alternately, something after the manner of school boys when they make up their sides to play a game of baseball. Captain Number One had the first choice, and then his opponent, and so on, until the two companies were made up. These preliminary matters having been arranged, they then set in to shucking corn.

The reader will remember that there are two piles of corn of equal size, and now there are two companies of shuckers of equal numbers, each company having a captain. It was considered no little honor to be elected captain of a corn-shucking company. His hat or cap was invariably decorated with the inside shucks of a large ear of corn. He was delighted with the office, and everybody—white and colored—did him honor. In the election of these captains, regard was had to their ability to sing: for the captains usually led their company in singing while shucking corn. At a given signal, each captain took his seat on the top of his pile of corn, and his shuckers surrounded it. While they shucked corn, they engaged in singing corn-shucking songs. Much of the fun of the occasion depended upon which side should win. It was a race that grew more exciting as the piles of unshucked corn grew less. They shucked, they sang, and they shouted. Then they knew that a bountiful supper awaited them just as soon as the work was done. On they went—a jolly good set, singing, joking and laughing. In the midst of it all, they could sniff the aroma of hot coffee, and the delicious odor of roasted meats and other nice dishes. This, as well as the hope of victory, was quite an inspiration to the boys. Well, the work is done. The last ear of corn has been shucked, and captain number one, with his company, has won. See the boys, as they toss their hats into the air! Hear them shout! The victory is theirs. They are a happy set.

Supper is now ready. Long tables—well laden with good things—have been prepared. Fully two score colored women are there to wait on the table. And they eat, and eat, and drink, to their satisfaction. The supper being over, with the moon shining brightly (moon-light nights were invariably selected for corn-shuckings) the boys spend some time in wrestling, foot racing and jumping before going home. And in all these games they matched one's agility, strength, and manhood against that of his fellow. This is kept up until a late hour of the night, and then they retire to the various plantations whither they belong.

Such was the corn-shucking on the old plantation in ante-bellum days. It was very much enjoyed by both the white folks and the slaves. The incidents and the happenings of a corn-shucking were long talked of on all the plantations represented. Nearly all the plantations had their corn-shuckings, and they certainly kept things lively during this season of the year in those days.

CHAPTER XI.

Little Jimmie, the Mail Boy, on the Old Plantation.

Little Jimmie was, perhaps, the most interesting character on Mr. Frierson's plantation. He was not a mulatto in the strict sense of that word. Webster, who is an authority on the meaning of words in the English language, says: "A mulatto is the offspring of a negress by a white man, or of a white woman by a negro." Jimmie was the son of Uncle Tom and Aunt Namie. Both of them were mulattoes. Both of their fathers were white and both of their mothers were black.

Jimmie's father—Uncle Tom—was a free man. He was born a slave, but purchased himself and his mother long before the first gun of the Civil War was fired. He was a man of industry, frugality, and wisdom. His wife—Aunt Namie—possessed the same qualities as her husband in an eminent degree, to all of which she added another very desirable quality, and that was a deep and sincere piety. Though a slave, she was one of Zion's noblest daughters.

Jimmie was not like Isaac, a child of promise; nor like Moses, a goodly child; nor like Samuel, a child of desire and prayer; but like the unnamed offspring of David and Bathsheba, he was a child of affliction. According to the testimony of his mother, his father, and his grandmother, he came into the world a sorely afflicted child. They never thought that they would ever succeed in raising the little fellow. But they did all in their power for the child, backed by the efforts of the white folks; and God blessed the means used, and the child lived, and grew to be a bright and active little boy.

Jimmie possessed a lively, sunshiny, and frank disposition, which never failed to win friends for him. Consequently, from his early childhood, he became a general favorite on the plantation among both the white folks and the slaves. Just as soon as he became old enough, his old master took him from his mother to be his waiting-boy. This necessitated his eating at the yard and sleeping in the white folks' house. Family prayers were invariably had, evening and morning, and Jimmie was always called in. The family sat in a semi-circle around the fireside, and Jimmie's little chair formed a part of that semi-circle. The Bible was read in a most impressive manner, and prayer was offered. The memory of those days has always been helpful and a source of inspiration to Jimmie.

But Jimmie had many narrow escapes from death. In the big house, he slept on a pallet before the fire. One night, between midnight and day, his bed took fire. And, strange to say, it burned some considerable time before he realized what was the trouble. It is true, he felt the fire, but, in his sleep, he imagined himself being toasted by a big oak fire on a cold winter's night. However, he awoke, and to his utter astonishment, found his bed to be on fire. He aroused himself and tried to put the fire out, but failed. By this time the large room was filled with smoke, which became stifling. One of the young ladies—Miss Mary Ann—awoke, and asked if his bed was not on fire, and Jimmie told her, "Yes." She told him to take it out into the yard, which he did. He then applied water, and put it out. He sat up the balance of the night, but, like a shipwrecked seaman, he wished for the morning.

When Jimmie was about twelve years of age, he had a narrow escape from death by drowning. It was the custom among the slaves—both men and boys—to go in swimming after dinner. The place was a deep lake on the stream called Pudden Swamp. Up to this time Jimmie had not learned how to swim. The edge of the lake was shallow, but as you advanced toward the centre, it became deeper and deeper until it reached perhaps some twelve or fifteen feet. The boys of Jimmie's age and size bathed near the banks, while the men, and those who could swim, plunged into the deep. Once Jimmie ventured too far out, and got into water where he could not touch bottom. Down he went: and when he arose, he screamed. This attracted the attention of all who were in bathing. He sank again, and when he came up the second time, his oldest brother Sam, who was an expert swimmer, caught him and saved him. Thus he was rescued, through the mercy of God, from a watery grave. Had this occurred on an occasion when these men were not present (for the boys often went in swimming without them) Jimmie would certainly have been drowned.

This boy was full of mischief, and reckless daring. He would venture to ride wild horses, unbroken mules, and even untamed steers. Once, while riding the little mule Jack, he was thrown with violence and tremendous force to the ground. It nearly killed him. After lying there awhile, he came to, and got up, but no traces of the little mule could be seen. In after years, Jimmie thought on these narrow escapes from death, and took comfort in the saying of an old writer: "Second causes do not work at pleasure. This is the bridle that God has upon the world." Lack of space prevents the writer from recording, in detail, all the miraculous deliverances from death, which marked the life of this much favored youth.

Jimmie was something of a privileged character on Mr. Frierson's plantation. It is true, he had to work in the field along with the other hands. Sometimes he dropped corn and peas; sometimes he thinned corn and cotton; and sometimes he hoed or plowed. But when Mr. Frierson would go off on business in his buggy, Jimmie had to go along and drive him. When his daughters went to church, or to make social calls, he went to drive them, and to care for the horses. So Jimmie had the privilege of attending all the big meetings, the weddings, and the parties of the white folks. All this proved to be of considerable advantage to him in gaining knowledge and information. Frequently on his return from some of these trips, the slaves would gather around him—old and young—to hear him tell what he saw and heard. And for days these things would be discussed by the body of slaves. This helped also to break the monotony of plantation life.

But as Jimmie grew up to young manhood, he became an expert horseman. There were none on the place, even among those older than he, white or colored, who could surpass him in this particular. His old master—Mr. Frierson—was so well pleased with Jimmie's achievements along this line that he gave him a pony named Charlie. This horse was a chestnut sorrel, with a star in his forehead, and a double mane, or a mane that fell gracefully on both sides of his neck. He was built exactly like a race horse. His body was long and slim, and his legs long and slender. His tail was of medium length, and inclined to be bushy. Jimmie ran many a race with Charlie, and had him so thoroughly trained that no horse or mule on that plantation, or on the adjoining plantations, could run with him. It was Jimmie's duty—in addition to the work he did on the farm—to go twice a week—Wednesdays and Saturdays—to Mr. Chris Player's, two miles away, for the mail, and to bring up the cows and sheep. Hence Jimmie never made a full hand on the farm, but worked when he was not needed for other duties.

But there is another interesting incident in the life of this youth, which the author cannot fail to relate. It occurred when he was about fifteen years of age. In the spring of 1865 the War between the States ended. The result was, all the slaves became free. A contract was signed by master and slaves to remain together the balance of that year and finish the crop.

It was now in the fall of that year, and the crops were being gathered. The children and young folks were sent to the field to pick peas. Jimmie was one of the number. The field was in sight of the white folks' house. From this house the white folks had a splendid view of these youngsters. They worked tolerably well until toward sundown, when they became very playful and frolicsome. From the house, the white folks saw their pranks. But nothing was said, yet they noticed that young "Mas" Dolphus was coming toward them with his double-barrel shotgun on his shoulder. They suspected nothing; but supposed that he was going on a squirrel hunt, as he was wont to do in the cool of the afternoons. As a matter of course, the youngsters all sobered down to work—seeing "Mas Dolphus" coming. And not a word was spoken, until he walked right up to Jimmie, and drew from under his coat a long whip, and began to lay it on him. The young master uttered these awful words as he continued to hit Jimmie: "Run if you dare, and I'll blow your brains out." Of course, the sight of the gun, and the threatening words of the young master had a decided effect in taming this young freedman. He stood and took it as good naturedly as he possibly could. And when he had gone the rounds (for he gave all a little) and left, Jimmie said: "I am not going to take this: for I am going straight to Sumter, and report this fellow to the Yankees." Brave words these! for a boy of fifteen, who was born and bred a slave, and taught nothing but to obey. He left the field immediately, jumped over into the swamp, went around the plantation, entered his mother's house, got his Sunday clothes, and struck out for Sumter, twenty-five miles away. He was followed by a boy called Henry, who was six months his junior, but was somewhat larger in stature. Henry had never been more than five miles from home in his life, and knew nothing but to work. Hence, it will be seen that Jimmie's traveling companion was not calculated to encourage him very much.

From the white folks, Jimmie had learned that the slaves were all free, and that the country had been put under military government. From them he learned that there was a garrison of Union soldiers in the town of Sumter, and that there was a provost marshal there, who heard and settled difficulties between the freedmen and their former owners. It was a knowledge of these things that prompted him to do what he did.

Jimmie and Henry left the old plantation just about dark. They told nobody of their departure, not even their mothers. How it must have pained them, when they discovered, at supper time, that these boys came up missing. Those were critical times. The war had just closed, but the country was still infested with lawless wanderers, who did not hesitate to commit crimes of all kinds. Robberies and murders were quite common. But in the face of all this, they plunged into a long, dark, and dense woods. Jimmie did not know the way to Sumter by the way of the State road, though he had traveled it several times with the white folks. But he knew that the railroad coming from Wilmington, N. C.—which ran within twelve or fifteen miles of Mr. Frierson's place—and going to Kingville, S. C., went by Sumter: for farmers from that section always crossed it near Sumter, going into the town. Now, Jimmie's plan was, to get to the railroad, and then following the track in a westward direction, they would be sure to reach Sumter. And, after persuing their journey through these fifteen miles of black forest, they struck the railroad about 11 o'clock in the night. Jimmie at once suggested to Henry that they camp for the night. It was agreed to. So they crossed the railroad, and went about a hundred yards, raked up some pine straw and oak leaves, and lay down to sleep close by the side of each other. They slept as quietly and as sweetly as two little fawns. Sometime during the night, Jimmie was aroused by a passing train. As he raised up, and saw its glaring headlight, and heard its thundering noise, which shook the earth beneath him, he was so terribly frightened until he could not call Henry. The next morning he asked Henry if he heard or saw the train in the night, and he said, "No."

They arose betimes, and began their long journey for Sumter. They had no breakfast. In fact, they had had no supper the night before. They left home so unceremoniously until they forgot to take provisions for the journey. It is needless to say that they left in great haste: for such was the case. They had no money, and knew nobody by the way, and yet they did not steal. They reached Sumter, and found their way to the provost marshal's office before he came down. And, to their surprise, they met a crowd of other colored people there, who, like themselves, had had difficulties with their former owners, and came from all parts of the country, seeking redress. They were heard one at a time. And when these boys' turn came, they entered the office as timidly as a hare. This was their first sight of a Yankee soldier in uniform. There were two of them, but the boys could not remember their names. When Jimmie and Henry were asked in a most tender manner what they wanted, the former's heart was so touched, until he burst into a flood of tears. But when his tears were brushed away, Jimmie rehearsed the whole matter to them. This was his first public speech, and he never forgot it. The officers asked the boys if they had parents, and they told them, "Yes." But Jimmie told them that his father was a free man, and was living on a rented farm to himself. The provost marshal wrote him a note—telling him that his son was now free, and that he must take care of him, and not allow him to return to the old plantation. This was done. Henry was given a letter to Mr. Frierson, which he took back to him, and was not molested.

CHAPTER XII.

A Love Story on the Old Plantation.

This love story is not a tale of fiction, nor is it one of romance, but it is a real story of love based on facts. It contains all the elements necessary to the making of a fascinating novel of two hundred or more printed pages. The characters were both slaves—having been born and reared in that condition. Nevertheless, they were not so lowly as to escape Cupid's notice. He aimed a dart at the heart of each of them, and in each case it struck and stuck fast. The flame that was kindled in these hearts by the son of Mars and Venus was as pure, and burned as fervently as in any human breast.

Jimmie, the bright little mail boy, fell in love with Isabella. This young girl was a beautiful quadroon. She was inclined to be tall, and somewhat slim, and possessed a lovely face. Her skin was fair, her eyes were dark, and her hair was black and fell in curls upon her shoulders. Her teeth were white, and it seemed that nature took special pains in making them in a uniform size, and in adjusting them in such a way that they would be attractive, and an object of admiration to all with whom she came in contact. Her dresses were always neat and clean. They were such as were worn by the nurses and chambermaids of the well-to-do white folks of that day and time. This beautiful girl—Isabella—belonged to Mr. Charles Durant, who lived on Lynches river, about five miles above Lynchburg, on the main road to Bishopville. This put a space of some twelve miles or more between Jimmie and his lover. And while he loved her dearly, yea, with all his heart, yet he could not go to see her. The distance was too great, and he was too shy and young. Therefore he had to wait until the spring season, when the quarterly meeting took place at the Methodist church at Lynchburg, or until the fall, when the annual camp-meeting was held at the old Tabernacle camp ground on Lynches river about four miles below Lynchburg.

As already stated, the Methodist parsonage was located at Lynchburg, and, perhaps, the largest and most important church of the circuit was at this point. And when the quarterly meeting of this church took place, it brought together many people from different parts of the circuit, and among them were the Friersons and the Durants. It was here that Jimmie would have the privilege of meeting his sweetheart—Isabella.

She was nurse and waiting maid for the Durants, and was invariably brought along to care for the baby. Jimmie was coachman, and came as driver for the Frierson girls. While the services would be going on in the church, and the minister would be delivering one of his most eloquent discourses to an intensely interested audience, Jimmie and Isabella would be sitting out in the carriage talking love, and making plans which they could never be able to execute. Being slaves—and quite youthful at that—there were insurmountable barriers in the way, which they did not dream of. But it was a great pleasure for them to meet on these big meeting occasions, and look at each other, smile at each other, and tell each other how much each loved the other. One did not doubt the sincerity and genuineness of the other's love. Each felt that their love was reciprocated, and this, in a measure, gave them satisfaction. These quarterly meetings lasted only about two days—Saturday and Sunday—and thus ended the interviews of Jimmie and his beloved Isabella. These meetings usually were held every three months on the charge, but in the Lynchburg church it took place in the spring of the year, and these lovers would meet no more until the fall, when the great Tabernacle camp-meeting came on.

The location of this camp ground has already been mentioned. The annual camp-meeting was a great occasion. Everybody went to camp-meeting—white and colored. Many of the prominent farmers connected with the Lynchburg circuit, were tent-holders at this camp ground. Mr. Frierson and Mr. Durant had tents on the same line. These tents were built of pine lumber, and in cottage style. They were built with several rooms, and with front piazzas. They formed a large circle, with the tabernacle, or church, in the center. Elevated scaffolds, about three feet square, with earth thrown up on them, and a bright lightwood blaze burning on the top, constituted the lighting system of the encampment. In addition to these scaffold-lights, there were bonfires built on the ground in front and in the rear of each tent. All culinary work was usually done at this fire in the rear.

When the trumpet would sound, which was a signal for the commencement of the services at the tabernacle, and when the white folks and the more serious servants and slaves would repair thither for worship, Jimmie would go over to Mr. Durant's tent, and spend the evening with his beloved Isabella, or at least until services at the tabernacle were out. This was done each evening, while the camp-meeting lasted, which usually was five or six days. These camp-meetings were great occasions. In fact, they were the biggest occasions that came within the experience of plantation life, and were hugely enjoyed by all, white and colored, old and young, male and female.

The last camp-meeting that Jimmie and Isabella attended was in the fall of 1864. The following year the white people who owned Isabella moved away to parts unknown to Jimmie. Hence he gave up all hope of ever seeing his lover again, and doubtless Isabella did the same. But while the sacred flame of love burned down, it was never completely extinguished.

In the fall of 1865, as has already been stated in a previous chapter, Jimmie left the old plantation, and went to the Yankees at Sumter. The provost marshal returned him to his father, who lived on a rented farm near Lynchburg. Here Jimmie worked on his father's farm during the summer months, and went to school at Lynchburg in the winter. After completing the course in this school, his father sent him to a school of a higher grade at Sumter. About this time Jimmie was converted, and became a Christian. He also felt that he was divinely called to preach the Gospel to his people. Consequently his father sent him to Charleston, S. C., to study divinity in the Baker Theological Institute, and afterwards to Claflin University at Orangeburg.

In December, 1870, at the age of 20, he joined the South Carolina Conference of the Methodist Episcopal Church, and was sent to Cheraw. He arrived at this historic old town on a Saturday night, and was met at the station by one of the officers of his church by the name of Johnson. This brother accompanied the young pastor to his own home, where he spent the night.

The next morning, which was the Sabbath, the young preacher repaired to the church in company with Brother Johnson. There was a large congregation present to see, and hear the new preacher. Expectation, born of genuine curiosity, was at its height. This was true of both the people and the preacher.

At the close of the services, the people—both the brothers and the sisters—gathered around the chancel to become acquainted with the new pastor, and to extend to him a warm welcome. Among the sisters, who came forward, Jimmie noticed one who exhibited traces of having been a most beautiful woman. She was tall, with fair skin; dark eyes, and straight black hair. But Jimmie also noticed that her teeth had been shattered, and some of the front ones were gone.

But he suspicioned and suspected nothing. Jimmie was an innocent and inexperienced young fellow. But this woman, like every other member of her sex, possessed a woman's instinct. While the other folks withdrew from the altar, she still lingered, and once more brought herself face to face with the young stranger.

Then she ventured to say to him: "I think I have met you somewhere before." "I do not remember," said the young pastor. "But where are you from?" said the woman. "Lynchburg is my home," answered the preacher. "Well, please pardon me, were you ever a slave?" asked the fair inquirer. "I was," he replied. "Well, to whom did you belong?" she asked. "I used to belong to the Friersons on Pudden Swamp." "Well, please tell me what might be your first name." "My first name is James, but all my friends call me 'Jimmie.'" "Oh, don't say so!" she said, excitedly, while her beautiful black eyes filled with tears. She then gently dropped her head, and wiped her eyes with a handkerchief that was well saturated with cologne. When she had succeeded in getting her face straight, she looked up and said in a very familiar way, "Jimmie, don't you know me?" He replied, "I can't say that I do." Then came the astounding words, "I am Isabella, that used to belong to Mr. Charles

Durant." Jimmie was stricken with dumbness, and when he became able to break the silence, all he could say was: "Well, well, well." It is needless to say that they were glad to see each other: for their joy was inexpressible. For a few moments, while they stood there, they gave a brief account of their whereabouts during the six or seven years since they last met at the old tabernacle camp ground. During this period Isabella had married, and she and her husband both were members of Jimmie's church.

About this time, he met a young woman of education, a successful school teacher, whom he courted and married. She was born of free parents, and reared in one of the large cities of the South. She is a woman of deep piety, and sustains a high moral standard. She is a great church worker, and much of Jimmie's success in the ministry has been attributed to the aid she has given him. She has proved herself to be a helpmeet indeed. Isabella was beautiful, but was not a woman of education, and therefore could not have filled the bill, and God knew it, and, in His wisdom, ordered otherwise. In discussing this matter, Jimmie has often been heard to repeat the lines:

"In each event of life, how clear
Thy ruling hand I see!
Each blessing to my soul more dear,
Because conferred by thee."

But all through life Isabella continued to show a fondness for Jimmie. Some years after this, she moved away to the Land of Flowers, and, as an evidence of her friendship for him, she shipped him a crate of beautiful Florida oranges. Since that they have lost sight of each other.

N. B.—Since the above chapter was written, Jimmie, in his wanderings, chanced to meet a sister of Isabella, and from her he learned that she (Isabella) moved from Florida to New Jersey, where she died. Thus ended the earthly career of a beautiful woman, and a lovely character. But Jimmie is still alive, and is doing active work as a gospel minister.

CHAPTER XIII.

The Breaking Up of the Old Plantation.

On the morning of April 12th, 1861, the first gun of the great Civil War was fired. It was fired on Fort Sumter from a Confederate battery located in Charleston harbor. It was a terrific bombardment of thirty-four hours' duration. This was the beginning of a struggle which resulted in the emancipation of 4,000,000 of slaves. On the 1st day of January, 1863, President Abraham Lincoln issued his famous Emancipation Proclamation, and it completely swept away the institution of African slavery, which had had an existence on the American continent for two hundred and forty-four years. But this Proclamation did not go into universal effect until General Lee surrendered at Appomattox Courthouse on the 9th of April, 1865.

At this time—April 9th—the farmers in the South had pitched their crops. The corn, the cotton, and the potatoes had been planted, were up, and growing nicely. And now comes the emancipation of all the slaves, and if they all leave the old plantation at once, what would be the result? It meant starvation and death both for the white folks and the newly made freedmen. But the authorities at Washington relieved the situation by advising the landlords and the ex-slaves to enter into contracts to remain together until the following January, to work the crops, and to divide them at the harvest in the fall. This was done.

We come now to the most pathetic part of our story, namely: "The Breaking Up of the Old Plantation." And well do I remember it. I do not remember the day of the week—whether it was Monday, Tuesday, or some other week-day—but most vividly do I remember the scene.

Mr. Frierson—on a certain day—requested all the hands on the plantation to come to the "house." The men, the women, and the children were included in his order. And some of the free colored people of the neighborhood heard of the order, and they also came to see and hear. In those days of excitement, curiosity reached a high degree of feverish expectation and desire for knowledge, for information, and for light. The slaves had heard of the Emancipation Proclamation, which had been issued a little more than two years before, but which had never changed their condition. They had also heard of the surrender of General Lee, which put an end to the war. Mr. Adolphus—a Confederate soldier—had returned home, and there he sat at a small table on the front piazza, writing. The paper which he was writing afterwards proved to be the contract between the landlord and the ex-slaves, which they were called together to sign.

It was a beautiful spring day. There was not a cloud in the heavens to obscure the brightness of the sun. The yard in front of the piazza, and in front of the east end of the same, was crowded with negroes. Their faces were all turned toward Mr. Frierson, who stood on the piazza with the contract in his hand. Their eyes were fixed on him, and their ears were attentive. But before he read the contract, he made to them a speech. He spoke, in part, as follows:

"My Servants: I call you together today, to read this contract to you, and have you all to sign it. This is the order issued by the Government at Washington. The North and the South have been engaged in a four-years' bloody war. As you all know, I have had two sons at the front—your Marse Rush and your Marse Adolphus. Your Marse Rush was killed in battle by those cruel Yankees, and is buried in an unknown grave in that far off land. Your Marse Adolphus—through a kind Providence—passed through the awful struggle without receiving as much as a scratch, and has been permitted to return home to us again. I know you all are glad, and rejoice with me in his safe return.

"But I must now tell you that you all are no longer my slaves. All the colored people who have been held in the South as slaves are now free. Your freedom is one of the results of the war, which has just closed. I do not know what you all are going to do after this year. I do not know whether you intend to leave me, and go out to seek homes elsewhere, or whether you will remain. But I want to assure you that I will be glad to have you all remain—every one of you.

"There is not one among you that was not born in my house, save four, namely: Uncle Fridie and his wife, and Uncle Isom and his wife. These four came into my possession by inheritance. They were my father's slaves, and when he died, at the division of his estate, they fell to me. I have kept them through all these years, even down to old age. And when they became so old and feeble that they could not work, I have kindly clothed, fed and cared for them. I have made them as comfortable in their declining years as it was possible for me to do.

"Then again, I declare unto you that I have not been cruel to any of you. I have not abused you myself, and did not allow anybody else to do it—not even my own sons, Mack, Rush, nor

Adolphus. And all the neighborhood knew that I did not wish to have my negroes imposed upon. The patrols so understood it. And to avoid trouble with them, and to keep them from slashing your backs when they caught you away from the plantation, I always wrote you a ticket or a pass. But some of you have gone off without my knowledge, and without a ticket, and have been caught and whipped, but it was not my fault. I was not to blame for that. You, yourselves, were responsible for it.

"There is another thing which I want to call your attention to. I have never put an overseer over you, neither have I employed a 'nigger driver' on my plantation. I have owned no blood hounds, and have not given any encouragement, nor employment to those who have owned them. I have never separated, by selling nor by buying, a mother and her child; a husband and his wife. Of the truth of this, you will bear me witness. In all these matters, I have the approval of a good conscience.

"And now, I wish to say again, you are no longer my slaves, but you all are now free. And I want to say to you that I bear no ill-will toward you. You are not responsible for the great change that has come upon us, and for the separation of master and servants. Others are responsible for these things. In the future let us be friends and good neighbors. You all have been taught to work, and to behave yourselves, and I hope you will continue to lead such lives in the future."

At the close of this talk, Mr. Frierson read the contract, in which it was agreed that all the slaves should remain on the plantation until the first day of January, 1866, when the crop would be divided. When he had finished reading, the older heads of these ex-slaves filed in one by one, and touched the pen in the hand of Mr. Adolphus, and made their mark. They then left the yard, and returned to their work.

But what were their feelings? Ah! words are inadequate to describe them. Their joy was unspeakable. But they had good sense. They imagined what were the feelings of the white folks because of the loss of their slaves. They knew that they were chafed in their minds, and that an outward demonstration of joy on their part would be unwise. Therefore their rejoicing was a subdued rejoicing. Though they had been kindly treated, and their relations to, and their attachment for, the white folks had been one of tenderness, yet they welcomed the change, and were glad of the new order of things. But they scarcely knew what it all meant. It was decidedly a new experience to them. They all remained except Jimmie until January.

During the fall the crops were harvested and divided according to the provisions of the contract, and when January came, there was a breaking up, and a separation of the old plantation. Nearly all the slaves left and went out and made contracts with other landlords. A few remained for one year, and then the last one of them pulled out and made their homes elsewhere. Thus they were all scattered, as it were, by the four winds of the heavens, never to come together again until the judgment.

Sometime during the next spring (1866) Mr. Frierson, the proprietor of the old plantation, went out into the field to view his growing crop, and fell with a paralytic stroke, and died soon after. He was buried at the old family graveyard.

In 1886, just twenty years after the breaking up and separation of the old plantation, Jimmie, the mail boy, (now the Rev. ———) returned to Lynchburg to visit his parents—Uncle Tom and Aunt Namie. It was during this visit that Jimmie proposed to his mother that they visit once more the Friersons' at the old plantation on Pudden Swamp. He thought he discovered in himself a sorter hankering desire to revisit the place where he first saw the light, and view once more the scenes of his childhood. He had heard that Mr. Frierson—the old man—had gone to his long home, so had Mr. Adolphus, but the girls were still living, and occupied the old mansion on the Frierson plantation, and Jimmie wanted to see them once more in this life. Hundreds of times Jimmie had driven those girls in the carriage while attending "big meetings," weddings, and while making social calls. In those days these girls were good to Jimmie, and he had not forgotten it. Now, he wants to see them for the last time, so he persuaded his mother to accompany him to the old plantation. This she readily consented to do.

After breakfast one morning Jimmie hitched up his father's horse and buggy and, with his mother, started for Pudden Swamp. They drove up into the yard at the Friersons' just as the old clock in the "house" struck 12, and Jimmie recognized the familiar tones of the old timepiece, and it so filled him with glee that as he alighted from the buggy, he said: "That is the same old clock by which I used to rise at four in the morning, and blow the horn for the boys to come and feed the horses and the mules." And so it was.

But the girls were filled with surprise. They did not recognize Jimmie. They recognized the woman who was with this young stranger. They knew Aunt Namie very well. They had seen her several times since she left the old plantation. This was not the first time that she had visited them, and once or twice the girls had driven up to Lynchburg to see Aunt Namie. These girls loved Aunt Namie, and Aunt Namie loved them, and it was their delight to visit each other, and talk over old times.

When this young stranger helped Aunt Namie from the buggy, the white girls rushed up to her and kindly greeted her. It certainly was a warm meeting. Jimmie then proceeded, as they used to say on Pudden Swamp, "to loose out the horse." And while doing so, he carefully watched the women folks as they embraced each other, but he had nothing to say. But the girls were pondering the expression which they heard this young stranger make as he drove up into the yard: "That is the same old clock by which I used to rise at 4 o'clock in the morning, and blow the horn for the boys to come and feed the horses and the mules." They closely eyed him, but there was nothing about him that would enable them to detect him. He was well dressed, and had an air of refinement about him which they were not accustomed to see about the male darkies on Pudden Swamp, notwithstanding they had been free for upwards of twenty years.

Now, the girls ventured to ask: "But, Aunt Namie, who is this man you have with you?" Aunt Namie replied: "Why, Miss Mary Ann, you don't know who that is?" "No," was the response. "Why," said Aunt Namie, "that is my little Jimmie, don't you know him." "Aunt Namie," said Miss Mary Ann, "do you mean to say that that is Jimmie, our little mail boy and our coachman?" "Yes, that is Jimmie." "Come here, Jimmie," said the girls, "give us your hand. How glad we are to see you. How have you been all these years?" This was another glad meeting. The balance of the day was spent as a reunion of the members of a family long separated.

The ladies showed Jimmie where to give the horse water, and where to feed him. Then they invited Aunt Namie and Jimmie into the house. Dinner was about ready, and a side table was set in the dining room for the visitors. It was the same old dining room, and it was a real good old-fashion farmer's dinner. Aunt Namie and Jimmie enjoyed it immensely.

After dinner, Jimmie left his mother and the girls to spend the afternoon talking about old times, while he alone roamed over that old plantation. From field to field he went, without seeming to grow weary, observing and noting every change. He noticed that the fences, the gates, the bars, and the bridges over the ditches were all gone. And in many places the fields had grown up with undergrowth and looked like woods again. "Ah," said Jimmie, "how cruel old Time is. He has laid his decaying hand upon everything on the old plantation. That which he has not destroyed, he has left in a state of decay and ruin. The colored folks are all gone, and only two of the white folks are left to tell the sad story."

But there is one thing that interested Jimmie more than anything else, and that is the spot where he first learned to sin. Jimmie located the place as nearly as possible, owing to the changes which time had wrought in the face of the country. And when he had found it, he knelt down and prayed to the God of heaven, and asked forgiveness for all the sins that he ever had committed on the old plantation, or anywhere else, and then reconsecrated himself anew to God and to His service. Then he arose, and returned to the old mansion, and chatted with the girls until it was time for him and his mother to leave for home.

This last separation was a very sad one, for the reason that they all knew that they would never meet on earth again. And so it came to pass. They have all crossed the mystic river, save Jimmie, and have been gathered to their people on the other side. Tears were shed by all—white folks and colored folks—as they shook hands, and said, "Good-bye."

THE END.

APPENDIX.

Signs of a Better Day for the Negro in the South.

Being the Reprint of a Series of Articles Written for The Daily Record of Columbia, S. C., by Rev. I. E. Lowery.

I.

Introduction.

After consulting the editor of The Record, and obtaining his consent, the writer has concluded to write a series of articles on the subject, "Signs of a Better Day for the Negro in the South," and it is his wish that these articles be published in the Saturday afternoon's paper, so as to form a column of Sabbath reading for the members of his race. This article is intended to be an introduction to what is to follow.

"Signs of a better day for the negro in the South." But the negro reader will ask: "Are there any signs anywhere that foretell of a better day in the South for the negro?" And the writer answers, "Yes." The trouble with the majority of the colored people is, they look on the dark side of the picture too much. They read the daily papers and note the cases of lynchings, burnings, murders and the outrages committed on members of the race generally, and then they grow discouraged, and say the future of the negro in the South is dark, and is growing darker still. But not so, could he but read aright. First of all, the best white people of the South are opposed to these crimes being committed against the members of our race. The best and most influential papers of the South, both daily and weekly papers, are opposed to it, and they speak out in no uncertain sound against it. And what is the result? These crimes have gradually grown less. The facts prove that the brutal offense against the purity of womanhood has diminished, and the sickening crimes of lynchings, burnings, murders and outrages have largely decreased.

I herewith submit a clipping from a Northern paper:

"According to statistics, lynchings were fewer in 1909 than the year previous. Seventy-eight lynchings took place in the United States in 1909, a greater number than in any year since 1904, except 1908, with 100 summary executions. In 1907 there were 63, and in 1906 there were 72. The victims of the 1909 lynchings were 65 negroes and 13 whites. All but five negroes were in Southern States. Illinois and Oregon were the only Northern States to furnish instances of mob law last year, and two cases were recorded in the Territory of New Mexico.

"Virginia barely missed a record of 'no lynchings' in 1909. On Christmas day a mob at Hurley hanged a white man. Except for this tragedy, Virginia would have been the only Southern State with a clear record on lynchings for the year.

"In Oklahoma there was a quadruple lynching of cattle men, and there were several double lynchings in Southern States. Texas led with 13 cases and Georgia was a close second with 12.

"Crimes and alleged crimes against white women were the principal causes, and accusations of murder and theft were responsible for many cases. A charge of counterfeiting was the incentive in one case and kidnapping in another."

A careful reading of the above clipping will show that the crimes that incite to mob violence are not as numerous now as they have been some years in the past. This, evidently, is a sign of a better day for the negro in the South.

Not long since the writer was coming from Florence to Columbia. He passed through the gate at the union station into the yard where the trains stood on the several tracks. There was a stream of passengers following behind him. Some were white people, and some were colored. He heard the voice of some one inquiring of the gate keeper—in a joking way—if his ticket would take him to "Lynchburg," and on which track his train stood. Hearing the name "Lynchburg" called (which is a small station only 20 miles west of Florence), attracted the writer's attention; for it is the place of his birth. He turned to see the person who was speaking, and who was so good-natured, and so full of life—and at once he thought he recognized the individual and waited on the inside until he came through. He approached the stranger and said to him, "Sir, excuse me, but will you please tell me your name?" He said, "My name is E. D. Smith, junior United States senator from South Carolina." He then looked at the writer more closely and said, "Is this Irving Lowery?" and the reply was, "Yes." We were both born and raised at Lynchburg and played together when we were boys. We stepped inside and chatted pleasantly. Really we were boys again for a while.

Now, here are some of the things he told me. He first had something to say about 14 and 15 cents cotton. Everybody knows that that is Senator Smith's favorite theme. But he went on to say: "Lowery, the South is undergoing a change. She is getting out of her old grooves of thought and action. The motto of the South today is: Every man, irrespective of race or color, shall have a chance in the race of life." The writer, with his breast heaving with emotion, said: "Mr. Smith, is not this great change which has come over the South due to the young men and to the young women of the South?" and he answered, "Yes." Thus ended one of the most pleasant interviews the writer has ever had in his life. It is to be taken for granted that Senator Smith knows the South as well, or better, than any other man, for he travels all over the South, and he is in a position to speak for the South with authority. At any rate, his statement comes to the negro like good news from a far country and should fill him with hope and with aspiration, for there is a better day ahead of him right here in the land that gave him birth. Only let him cease from crime; let him be industrious, and let him educate his children and the white people of the South will see to it that he shall have fair chance in the race of life.

II.

White Patrons of Negro Business Enterprises.

The industrial achievements of the negro race in the South are signs of a better day. It is said by those who claim to know, that in the North the negro seldom engages in any independent business. Up there most of the colored population are cooks, chambermaids, nurses, laundry-women, butlers, coachmen, elevator boys and hotel waiters. This is all they can hope to be. Of course, there are some colored ministers up there, and here and there a lawyer, a physician and a few mechanics. But in the South the negro fills all of these minor and higher callings, and, in addition, he may become a farmer, a merchant, or even a college president.

I clipped the following from the editorial columns of The News and Courier, of Charleston, April 9th, 1907:

"In Charleston all the laundry wagons are driven by colored men, we believe. Nearly every delivery wagon sent out by the dry goods, grocery and other commercial establishments here is driven by a colored teamster. Nearly all the barbers in town are colored, many of them owning their own plants. There have been colored men on the Charleston police force for nearly forty years. There are also colored firemen employed here and paid by the city for their services. The drivers of the carriages of our best people are colored men. Quite a number of colored men are doing business here on their own account, and have been for years, and number among their customers many of the best white people in the town. There are four or five colored physicians practicing here. There are in Charleston, besides, colored lawyers and colored teachers. Many of the best dressmakers are colored women, and colored trained nurses are employed to attend white patients. There are also colored farmers, and one of the largest rose gardens in the South is owned by a colored man at Charleston. There are also in this town colored mechanics and colored contractors and colored labor unions. The most of the house servants employed in Charleston are colored, and now that the automobile microbe is infecting this community it is not an unusual sight to see these modern machines operated by colored chauffeurs."

It is true, and every intelligent person knows it, that every avenue of legitimate business is open to the negro in the South. And there is another thing that is true, and that is this: that it matters not what might be the nature of the business that a colored man may engage in, the white people, and the best white people, of the South, will patronize him. For instance, in Charleston, the butcher's business is largely controlled by colored men. This is true both in the down-town market and also in the green grocery business, as it is called, throughout the city. Gilliard & Fludd, T. S. Grant, John Stokien, Tom Marshall, the Hoffman Brothers, and Trescott, are among the leading colored butchers, and they do a large business, and serve some of the best white people of the city. C. C. Leslie, the colored fish merchant, did a fine business for nearly thirty years. He did a heavy business in supplying the local market, and shipped large quantities of fish to all parts of the State to both white and colored customers. Really, Leslie has become rich, and last year he sold out his business to a white man and retired, and is living in ease and comfort on his income.

Thaddeus Felon, of Summerville, owns a fine brick store near the Southern depot, in which he conducts a large dry goods store, employing colored girls as clerks, and the white people—gentlemen and ladies—trade with him. Of course he is making money. In this same town Dr. Allston practices medicine and conducts a livery business. Hoffman also conducts a livery business and runs a butcher shop. The Sasportas Brothers are butchers on a large scale. All of these colored business men have white friends who patronize their business liberally.

In Sumter, W. J. Andrews has been engaged in business for more than 30 years. He kept a first class restaurant for white and colored, having separate rooms for each race, and sold fish, oysters and ice. He did the largest business of this kind of any man in Sumter. He made money and is considered one of the wealthiest colored men of the town. He made the most of his money out of the white people, who thought that there was no negro in Sumter like "Bill Andrews." They believed him to be honest, industrious and truthful, hence they did not hesitate to trade with him. In Camden, Eugene Dibble is the best-to-do colored man of the town. When the writer visited that town last he owned and operated three stores and several farms. He is also the proprietor of several tenement houses. It is evident to the casual observer that this accumulation of property was not the result of colored patronage alone, but the facts show that much of it is the fruit of his white trade.

The city of Columbia has produced some successful colored business men, who have accomplished much through the patronage of their white friends. There was R. J. Palmer, who conducted a business as a merchant tailor on Main street nearly opposite the postoffice, and made money. "Cap" Carroll, as he was familiarly called by his friends (I mean C. R. Carroll), conducted an up-to-date white barber shop, and when he died he left his family in comfortable circumstances. He made his money out of the white people, and many of them, as well as hosts of colored people, regretted his death. And there is I. S. Leevy, a young man of intelligence and thrift, who is doing a good business as a tailor on Taylor street. He was educated at Hampton Institute in Virginia, where he learned the tailor's trade. He numbers some of the best white people of Columbia as his customers.

A few years ago, Charles Stewart, the noted negro newspaper correspondent of Chicago, was making a tour of the South, and spent a couple of days in Newberry. In his letter to The Afro-American Ledger, a negro journal, published in Baltimore, Md., he speaks as follows of some of the colored people of Newberry:

"We have some men in business here. T. A. Williams & Sons operate the grocery store right in the business section of the city and spitting distance of the court house. He owns 1,400 acres of land and some good property right in the city.

"G. C. Williams, who is brother to the one I have mentioned, owns 600 or 700 acres of land and is doing well. Robert Williams joins his brother, Thomas Williams, in owning and operating a brick yard; John D. Daniels perhaps is the leading meat man in town. It is said that he knows more about the meat business and has the largest trade. Some of the best white people in town buy meat from him. He also carries a full line of groceries, and is a property owner. W. W. Graham owns a grocery store, and is doing good business; A. G. Neeley is a young man in business. He has a grocery, and his wife is in charge of the business while he attends the farm. They are happy and are doing well. He owns some good property himself. Mrs. Mattie Neeley operates an eating house, and she does a good business, while her husband beats out iron. He is one of the leading blacksmiths of the town. He has as his partner, John Morgan, who knows how to operate, too."

In Anderson, a blacksmith, by the name of David Dooly, has earned and saved a small fortune. He works for the best white people of the town and county. He is skilled as a workman, is honest, truthful and perfectly reliable. He owns several good houses, and his note is good at any of the banks in town. But why go further in naming others, for men like these are found in almost every town and city in the South. Yes, there are colored men all over the South engaged in business and the white people do not hesitate to patronize them. They know that some of these negroes are making money, yet they are not envious, but trade right along with them, and thus help them up in the world. This is surely a sign of a better day for the negro in the South.

III.

White Contributors Toward the Building of Negro Churches.

There are thousands of white people in the South who contribute liberally toward the building of negro churches. This may be regarded as a hopeful sign of a better day for the colored people in the South.

During the days of slavery the colored people were connected with the churches of their masters. They were given the galleries, or a few seats at the rear end of the church, or, if they wanted to have their own services, the basement was given to them, and sometimes the main auditorium of the church proper was turned over to them when not in use by the white people. Thus all the slaves who were Christians in that day and time had their church home. Their master's church was usually their church. If he was a Methodist, his slaves were Methodists; if he was a Baptist, his slaves were Baptists; if he was a Presbyterian, his slaves were Presbyterians; and if he was an Episcopalian, his slaves were Episcopalians. It mattered not what church the master and his family were members of, the slaves usually belonged to the same.

But when freedom came, and when the newly made freedmen broke away from the "old plantation" and from their former masters, they left their church home behind them. They went out without spiritual leaders and without churches. They were as sheep having no shepherd and no fold. Just at this period of their history, the Northern missionary and the Northern school teacher came upon the scene. They had strong churches at their backs, which furnished them with money. These missionaries and teachers organized churches and established schools for the uplift of the negro. But it is not to be supposed that while the Northern white people did much the Southern white people did nothing. The truth of the matter is the benevolent and charitable work of the Northern white people have been magnified, while the same kind of work by the Southern white people has been minimized. In fact, no publicity scarcely has been given to the Southern white people. But now has not the time come to give the Christian white people of the South the honor due to them for their good and noble work in helping the colored people to better their condition? If justice was allowed to speak, she would answer "Yes."

But let us hear what Booker T. Washington, the greatest leader of the negro race, has to say on this subject. He says: "It may not be known outside of the South, and to the general public, but it is true that every branch of the Southern white church is assisting in some manner in the educational, moral and religious development of the negro through their college, Sunday school or church work. This country owes a debt of gratitude already to a group of brave, unselfish, courageous Christian white men and women in the South which it can never repay. It has been owing to the influence of this group, working in co-operation with the educated negro, that peace and harmony and good-will prevails in the South to the extent that it does. The future for both of our races is not dark."

I think the facts will bear me out when I make the statement that during the 45 years of our freedom there has not been a single church site bought nor a single church building erected anywhere in the South but what the Christian white people of the South put money into it. In addition to this, there are hundreds and thousands of cases, where Christian white men and white women of the South gave the land on which to build churches for colored people. Nor has the day of this mission work ceased. It is still being carried on all over the South today.

Now, I wish to give a few cases illustrating the fact that the Southern white people have helped and still are helping the colored people to secure sites and to build their churches. There is a remarkable case which occurred in the city of Charleston at the close of the Civil War. The history of this very interesting event was written by the Rev. W. H. Lawrence, a Northern white man, and published in a good-sized volume. The writer secured a copy of this book through the kindness of the Rev. James H. Holloway, a prominent member of this church. The historian says: "The history of the purchase of Centenary Church is an interesting evidence of God's care for His work. The people worshipping in the normal school early observed a day of fasting and prayer, that God would supply them with a suitable building. Bishop Baker heard of this touching instance of faith; he promised the brethren that the missionary society would assist them to secure a church. It was discovered that the Wentworth Street Baptist Church was for sale. This society had been so crippled by the war that it was determined to unite with the congregation worshipping at the Citadel Square Baptist Church. The Wentworth Street property is an elegant brick structure in the Corinthian style of architecture, with a fine lecture room attached. Its estimated value is $75,000.

"Negotiations were immediately begun, resulting in a bargain at $20,000. This amount the missionary society agreed to furnish. When the Baptist brethren discovered that their church was to fall into the hands of Northern brethren for the use of a colored congregation, they imposed further conditions, which seemed likely to prevent the sale. They said the money must be paid in gold, and during the banking hours of an appointed day. Gold commanded a premium of 50 per cent., which was an addition of $10,000 to the stipulated price. The Charleston people must raise this $10,000. Meetings were held, collectors appointed and an heroic effort made. Some of the mothers in Israel even contributed the money which had been sacredly laid away for their burial.

"As there was not $20,000 in available gold in the city, a broker was authorized to purchase this amount in New York. The box of precious metal reached Charleston on the morning of the day when the money must be paid, or the bargain broken. The broker declined the draft of $20,000 of the missionary society, which the brethren presented. Mr. Geo. W. Williams agreed to cash the draft, but as exchange then commanded a premium against the brethren, this involved an additional outlay of a few hundred dollars. Mr. Thomas Tulley and other well-to-do members of the church were fortunately able to command the needed amount. Mr. Williams' check was accepted by the broker, and a dray carried the box of gold to the lawyer's office, where the papers were to be signed. Just as the 2,000 golden eagles were being rung upon the counter the minute hand of the clock began to count off the last half hour of the appointed time, and the property passed forever into the hands of the Methodist Episcopal Church. The deed was made out, from motives of prudence, on account of the unsettled condition of the country, to the

Missionary Society of the Methodist Episcopal Church, to be held in trust by Alonzo Webster, Charles Holloway, George Shrewsberry, John Gibbs, Jacob Mills, Samuel Weston, January Holmes and Archibald Walker, trustees of the Methodist Episcopal Church in Charleston. This transaction took place on the 10th of April, 1866."

The point in the above piece of history, to which the writer wishes especially to call the reader's attention, is the part that Mr. Geo. W. Williams took in the delicate transaction. If he had not come to the rescue of this congregation and cashed that draft, these people never would have come into possession of that magnificent property on one of the principal streets of Charleston. Mr. Williams was a wealthy banker and was highly esteemed and reverenced by these people to the day of his death.

The church was bought in the centennial year of the establishment of Methodism, and therefore named Centenary. The Rev. M. M. Mouzon is the present pastor, and the Rev. Jas. H. Holloway is superintendent of the Sunday school. The church has 1,300 members and 600 Sunday school scholars.

IV.

White Contributors Toward the Building of Negro Churches.—(Continued.)

In my last article I spoke of the Southern white people as contributors toward the building of negro churches in the South. This I regard as a "sign of a better day." In that article I gave a history of the purchase of the Centenary Church in Charleston, which is considered one of the finest negro churches in the South, and the part that Mr. Geo. W. Williams—a wealthy banker—took in the transaction. But for him there would never have been a Centenary Church.

But in this article I wish to mention a few other cases where the colored people were assisted by their white neighbors. Take the Old Bethel M. E. Church, located on the north side of Calhoun street in Charleston. It is one of the oldest and most historic buildings in the city. It is certainly the oldest Methodist Church in the fair "City by the Sea." Bishop Asbury, the first bishop of Methodism, preached in the building now under consideration. It has been moved twice, but now it has reached perhaps its last resting place.

It is a substantial wooden building and well constructed. It was built in colonial days on the northwest corner of Pitt and Calhoun streets, the site where the new Bethel M. E. Church now stands. This is the church where Mr. F. J. Pelzer, a very wealthy gentleman, holds his membership. This old building stood on this corner lot for a number of years, during which time the congregation grew both in numbers and wealth. About this time they felt the need of a better and more modern building. This was long before the Civil War. They decided to erect a new brick building of Grecian architecture. A large number of colored people were connected with this church as members, and some of them were well-to-do free colored people. They occupied the gallery during the services.

Now, when these white folks were arranging to build their new church, they told the colored portion of the congregation that if they would give them $1,000 toward the erection of the new church they would roll the old one to the rear end of the lot and give it to them. The colored people were delighted and went to work to raise the money—both the slaves and the free colored people. The thousand dollars were raised, and the old building was shoved to the rear and fitted up. A beautiful new building took its place, which stands there today. The old building remained on its site until the close of the war, when the colored people went over to the

Methodist Episcopal Church. They also claimed the building, but they could not claim the land on which it stood. This belonged to the New Bethel congregation, and this congregation asked the colored people to move the building away, as they wanted the lot to erect a Sunday school room. They also promised the colored people to give them $500 to assist them in defraying the expense of moving the building. Luckily the colored people found a very desirable lot for sale just across the street (Calhoun) and they bought it. In the purchase of this lot there was something that the New Bethel congregation did not like, and they refused to carry out their agreement of giving the colored people $500 to help them. They thought that they had good and sufficient reasons for their decision in the matter, but Mr. Pelzer differed from them, and stood by the original agreement. He wrote his personal check for $500 and gave it to the colored people. The old building was moved and fitted up and called "Old Bethel." The writer had the honor of serving this church as pastor for six years not long since, and it was during this period that he made it his business to see Mr. Pelzer in person and get the facts from him. He gave them to me as related above. Mr. Pelzer is a good man, but he is not the only good white man in the South. There are thousands just like him. Are not incidents like this a sign of a better day for the negro in the South?

But let us consider some other cases similar to the one named above. During last year (1909) a destructive storm passed over the little town of Greeleyville on the Coast Line Railroad between Sumter and Lanes, and blew down every colored church in the place. The Rev. E. W. Stratton, a native of Columbia, is pastor of the M. E. Church, and he told the writer that the white people of Greeleyville gave him $100 to assist him in rebuilding his church. One white gentleman, a member of the Baptist Church, gave $50 of that amount. There is a colored Baptist Church in course of construction near Norway, in Orangeburg County. This is a station on the Seaboard Air Line Railway. A white gentleman contributed $100 toward the building fund of this church and endorsed a note at the bank for $200, given by the officers.

But take one more case. There is a colored Methodist Church in Spartanburg called "Silver Hill." The building is of brick and was erected just after the war in a very ordinary style, with a school room on the first floor and the church auditorium above. Some 15 years ago the Rev. C. C. Scott was sent there as pastor, and he undertook the tremendous job of remodeling the church. He began the work, but was removed before it was finished. The writer was sent to complete the work, and therefore had access to the financial records. These books showed that the white people of Spartanburg gave something over $500 to complete the work. Among the largest contributors were: Mr. John B. Cleveland, Capt. Montgomery, Mr. Converse and Mr. Twitchell. But a large number of the white citizens contributed in smaller sums.

These are sample cases, the like of which can be found throughout the South. If all the incidents of this nature, which have occurred since emancipation, could be written it would make a large volume of many thousand pages.

V.

White Contributors Toward the Building of Negro Schools.

In two articles I discussed what the white people of the South have done in helping the colored people to secure sites for their churches, and the assistance rendered them in erecting buildings thereon. But before leaving this line of thought, I wish to call the reader's attention to the schools designed for the education of the colored youth of the South. I do not refer to the common school system. These schools have been provided by the State. The buildings, such as they are, in most cases have been erected out of public funds, raised by taxation. Aside from the public schools located in the towns and cities there is not much being done for the education of the young negro. The terms are too short—lasting only from two to three months. This is a serious mistake, for the reason that it causes hundreds and thousands of some of the best colored families to leave the farms and move nearer to or into the towns and cities for the purpose of educating their children. Whereas if the rural schools were made better and the terms extended, the colored people would be more willing to stay on the farms. In that case the educational facilities of the country would measure up to the standards of the towns and cities, and this would make the negro farmer contented to stay where he is. These points are worthy of a careful consideration by the land owners of the South.

But at the close of the war the negroes of the South were without school houses, as they were without church buildings. But as their church buildings multiplied, they were used in many cases as school houses. Finding that the public school was insufficient for the education of their children, the colored people began to plant and build denominational or independent schools. And even in this the Southern white people have helped them. There is not a single denominational or independent negro school in the South but what the white people put money into it, and helped to build it. And they are still helping them along this line. Of course, the Northern people have done much and are still doing much, but in recent years they have begun to tighten the strings of their purses. They are not doing as much now as they have done in the past. They seem to be growing tired of the negro. They say he is a burden, and that they have carried him long enough. Hence each year there is a considerable falling off in the gifts of the Northern people. This is the universal testimony of those who are engaged in the work of negro education under the patronage of Northern philanthropists. But it must be a pleasing thought to the close observer of passing events to note that while the donations of Northern people toward the education of the colored people are annually decreasing, those of the Southern white people are largely on the increase. The donations of the Southern white people are given, in most cases, to the secular or independent negro schools. I will now proceed to mention a few cases in South Carolina and some of the adjoining States.

Some time last fall it was the writer's privilege to visit the town of Marion. While there I spoke to the faculty and students of the colored graded school, and noticed that an additional new building on the campus was nearing completion. I was told by some of the colored people of Marion that that building was designed as an industrial building, and that it was the gift of Judge Woods, one of the Associate Justices of the Supreme Court of South Carolina. The information greatly impressed me, and I regarded it as a "sign of a better day for the negro in the South." But to be sure that the information given me by the colored people was correct, I wrote Mr. T. C. Easterling, the superintendent of the city schools of Marion, and this is what he said, touching that new building: "Our colored industrial school building and equipment cost something over $1,100. Of this amount Judge Woods was one of those who gave $200 each. The colored people themselves gave $132. The balance was given in amounts from $500 to $50. Nearly all of the white citizens of Marion to whom I went for money to build and equip our colored industrial school responded willingly." The above letter needs no comment, but I would, in passing, ask the reader to note the spirit of friendliness and charity on the part of the white citizens of Marion.

But one of the most conspicuous monuments of the charity of the Southern white people in the education of the negro is the Paine Institute, located in Augusta, Ga. The school was planted by the M. E. Church, South, and named after Bishop Paine, one of the great men of Southern Methodism. This school, which is one of the best in the South, established for the education of negro youth, is presided over by the Rev. George Williams Walker, D. D., a South Carolinian, a man of God, and a true friend of the colored man. He has devoted his best days to the uplift and the betterment of the colored people of the South. And thousands of the sons and daughters of Ham will rise up in the judgment and call him blessed. He deals with the hearts or morals of his pupils as well as with the intellects. When they pass through his school they do not only come out as educated young men and women, but they come out as Christians, prepared to fight the battles of life.

There is a school for the education of negro youth at Denmark, S. C. It was founded by a young colored woman by the name of Elizabeth Evelyn Wright. She was born at Talbotton, Ga., on April 3, 1874, and graduated from Tuskegee Industrial Institute, after which she came to this State. They have a magnificent plant of more than 380 acres of good farming land. These lands are dotted with five or six splendid buildings, which are well equipped for school purposes. The farm is well stocked with mules and cattle and abundantly supplied with the latest farming implements. A fine printing outfit has been installed. The school is supplied with a saw mill, and also a grist mill. The school plant is worth about $75,000 and is out of debt. Mr. Ralph Voorhees, of New Jersey, furnished the money to found this school, but it could not be done without the aid of the Southern white men. I will quote just one sentence from their latest catalogue, which will prove my statement: "Ex-Senator Mayfield, who lives at Denmark, became interested in her efforts, and has always been a friend to the work. He helped her to secure this large tract of land, and, all along, has he been a tower of strength in behalf of this negro school."

The Sterling Industrial College for negro youth is an independent or undenominational school located at Greenville, S. C., and the Rev. D. M. Minus, D. D., is the founder and president. Mrs. E. R. Sterling, of Poughkeepsie, N. Y., gave the first money to establish this school, therefore the school has been given her name. But Mrs. Sterling died soon after the school was founded, and the enterprise would have failed had not the white people of Greenville and Anderson come to its rescue. These good people have given thousands of dollars to the school, which kept it going, and have put it on a firm basis. I quote one paragraph from their recent catalogue:

"Its growth has been so rapid until in 1903 the trustees found it necessary to sell the old school site, on Choice street, and purchase larger and more convenient quarters in West Greenville, where better work, especially in the industries, can be done. The school has now a large farm, president's home with seven rooms, a main building containing 19 rooms, a large and comfortable dining hall, with other buildings, a magnificent park with splendid springs of pure water and large, open grounds for athletic purposes. With God's blessing and guidance and the hearty co-operation of our friends the school will increase as a powerful agency in educating and uplifting the young men and women of our race."

I have named only a few of the negro schools in the South that have been fostered by donations from the Southern white people. But similar schools are found in every Southern State from Virginia to Texas. Let the reader look, and see, and consider for himself.

VI.

Current Incidents of. Negro Industrial Achievements.

The industrial achievements under Southern conditions are a sign of a better day for the negroes in the South.

In January, 1866, the negroes left the old plantation with nothing—absolutely nothing. And they were ignorant, too. They had no education. They only knew how to work. They had been taught this in slavery. But recent statistics show a marvelous accumulation of property for a period of forty years. The figures are almost incredible, but they are said to be based on government authority. Here they are: They own 137,000 farms and homes, which consist of 40,000,000 acres.

These farms and homes are valued at $725,000,000. They have personal property to the value of $10,000,000. The different colored denominations own $41,000,000 of church, parsonage and school property.

But I wish to give two or three current incidents illustrating the possibilities of the negroes' success along industrial lines. But similar cases may be found everywhere in this beautiful Southland.

In Camden, S. C., there is a young man by the name of George Washington Clarke, who is a graduate of Tuskegee Institute, Booker Washington's school. This negro is employed by one of the wealthiest white gentlemen of that city as a gardener, or horticulturist, at a fine salary. He has charge of both his flower and vegetable gardens, and, as a result, this white citizen has a variety of nice, fresh vegetables the whole year round.

Not long since, the writer was traveling and came to a certain Southern city, and took the trolley cars for his boarding place. And when the car reached the junction, where all the cars came together at intervals, a young colored man walked in, got down on his knees and lifted a trap-door in the middle aisle, and made a thorough examination of the electric apparatus beneath the car. The writer saw that he was a car inspector, and when he had finished and walked out, he followed him, and asked his name and what salary he was paid. This information was willingly and freely given, but for prudential reasons, he requested that no publicity be made of it. But the fact is, the young negro was an electrician, and as such was given employment by a wealthy corporation right here in the South.

The wealthiest negro in the city of Atlanta, Ga., is A. F. Herndon. He owns and operates the largest barber shop in the city; is the president of a flourishing insurance company, and owns and rents some 50 dwelling houses. He is said to be worth $80,000, all of which has been made since the Civil War.

Bishop L. J. Coppin, D. D., of the A. M. E. Church, is considered one of the strongest and safest leaders of the colored race in America. In a recent lecture in Emanuel Church at Charleston, in speaking of the progress that the negroes are making in South Carolina, he said he saw in a white paper of this State that 55 per cent. of the farming lands of South Carolina is owned by colored people. The bishop said he could scarcely believe the statement, but he supposed that it was true, for these papers generally know what they are talking about. If it be true, said the bishop, it is certainly encouraging to the race.

To excel in any line of work is worthy of the effort. Alfred Smith, of Oklahoma, a negro, is put down as the champion cotton raiser. He has taken all the premiums offered in that State for the first and best cotton received, also the blue ribbon at the World's Fair, and the first prize in England. Smith is a native of Georgia, having been born near Atlanta, and claims that when Sherman passed through on his famous march to the sea, he was in the field plowing with an old gray mule. That this good brother should have continued at the plow until he is able to receive so many evidences of his ability as a cotton raiser, ought to be a source of inspiration to every negro in America. It shows that patient industry also has its reward.

Robert C. Owens, of Los Angeles, Cal., has been very fortunate in making investments in real estate. He began with a small capital as an option dealer, which has enabled him to amass property valued at the enormous sum of $675,000. He is a member of the Los Angeles Chamber of Commerce, and in a short time will have a monthly rent toll of $3,500.

VII.

Friendly Expressions of Southern White People for the Negro.

On February 26, 1910, the writer was in Aiken —having gone there to attend a farmers' conference. The early train from Augusta to Blackville was derailed at the freight depot, just on the outskirts of the town. Great crowds from the town and the surrounding country visited the scene of the wreck. Among these curious sightseers were several small boys—white and colored. It was Saturday, and, the schools being closed, the boys were on hand in full force.

Near the track was a hole about as large around as a barrel, and about as deep. This hole was nearly full of water, and there was a frog floating around in it. These boys soon lost interest in the wreck and gathered around the hole. They fished the frog out, and instantly a half dozen boys gathered up rocks and brickbats to kill it. They held in their hands missiles sufficient to kill a good-sized animal, with proper force behind them. The unanimous opinion of the boys was that the frog should be killed. Presently another little white boy came up and said: "Boys, what are you all going to do with that frog?" "Kill him!" cried a half dozen voices. "No, don't do that," said the newcomer. "That frog has as much right to live as any of you. Put him back in the hole and into the water." And, strange to say, this boy's advice was taken, and the life of the frog was spared. It was thrown back into its native element, the water.

"Now," said I, "there is the influence of one

voice when it pleads for the innocent and the helpless." This story may be applied to the negro and to his surroundings. There are voices that cry against him, but I am glad to say that there are some friendly voices that plead for him. In this, and in my next article, I purpose to mention some of these friendly voices.

The Atlanta riot is still fresh in the minds of the American people. It was a bloody affair, during which human lives were sacrificed and great damage done to the business of the city. Some days after the riot, the best citizens among the white people and among the colored held a mass meeting, in which frank and outspoken expressions were made. Some of these expressions I herewith reproduce.

Mr. Charles T. Hopkins, one of the ablest lawyers at the Atlanta bar, a native of Tennessee and a graduate of Williams College, made a speech at this meeting, in which he said: "The negro race is a child-race. We are a strong race, their guardians. We have boasted of our superiority, and we have now sunk to this level—we have shed the blood of our helpless wards. Christianity and humanity demand that we treat the negro fairly. He is here, and here to stay. He only knows how to do those things we teach him to do; it is our Christian duty to protect him. I for one—and I believe I voice the best sentiment of this city—am willing to lay down my life rather than to have the scenes of the last few days repeated."

In the same meeting a colored man arose to speak. He was timid and doubtful. It was Dr. W. F. Penn, one of the foremost colored physicians of Atlanta, and a graduate of Yale College. He said the mob went to his house to kill him, but he was saved by a white man, who spirited him away in an automobile. When he had finished, Col. A. J. McBride, a real estate owner and a Confederate veteran, arose and said with much feeling that he knew Dr. Penn, and that he was a good man, and that Atlanta meant to protect such men. "If necessary," said Col. McBride, "I will go out and sit on his porch with a rifle."

Ex-Governor W. S. Northen, one of the best known and most respected citizens of the State of Georgia, recently made an eloquent speech in that State in which he gave expression to these noble sentiments: "We shall never settle this (the race) question until we give absolute justice to the negro. We are not now doing justice to the negro in Georgia. Get into contact with the best negroes; there are plenty of good negroes in Georgia. What we must do is to get the good white folks to leaven the bad white folks, and the good negroes to leaven the bad negroes. There must be no aristocracy of crime; a white fiend is as much to be dreaded as a black brute."

Mr. Washington Gladden, in the January (1907) number of The American Magazine, says: "There are many Southern men who are determined that the negro shall not be reduced to serfdom; who mean that he shall have a chance to be a man—to make of himself what God meant him to be."

President Kilgo, of Trinity College, North Carolina, says: "The best Southern people are too wise not to know that posterity will judge them according to the wisdom they use in this great concern. They are too just not to know that there is but one thing to do with a human being, and that is to give him a chance."

Prof. Woodward, of the same college, says: "What is to be done with the negro race? It must somehow be built into this national fabric, and organically incorporated with the national life and character."

The Rev. Edgar Gardner Murphy, of Alabama, says: "While the development of the higher life of the negro may come slowly, even blunderingly, it is distinctly to be welcomed."

Senator B. R. Tillman, in a debate in the United States Senate on the discharge of the negro troops of the Twenty-fifth Infantry, who were summarily dismissed from the army by

President Roosevelt, said that there were many good negroes. He also said that he had had good negroes working for him 30 years, and he believed there were millions of good negroes.

Says Mr. Washington Gladden, in the January (1907) number of The American Magazine: "It is idiotic to talk of deporting the negroes to some other country; they are here, and here they must stay; and their home will be in the southern portion of the territory of the United States. Whether the two races shall live there together or live there separately is the only possible question. They cannot live together unless both races have full opportunity to live a complete human life."

These friendly expressions from some of the leading white men of the South are signs of a better day for the negroes in the South.

VIII.

Friendly Expressions of Southern White People for the Negro.—(Continued).

The friendly expressions of prominent Southern white men are signs of a better day for the colored people of the South.

The Rev. Samuel Phillips Verner—a young South Carolinian, who has consecrated his life to missionary work in Africa—pays an eloquent tribute to the devotion of his faithful black followers in that dark continent, and by this he was reminded of the fidelity of the slave to his master in this country. Ten of his devoted men sacrificed their lives that Mr. Verner's might be saved. He afterwards found an arm on the bank of the river, and only an arm, which told the sad story of their death in his defence. In speaking of this incident Mr. Verner says: "As I looked at it (the arm) through a mist of tears, there rose to mind another scene, a far off and happier land, but on a day of strife and battle, when, amid the cannon's roar and the shriek of the flying balls, an old man lay wounded and near to death. But a black arm encircled him, and bore him through the hell of battle raging around, safely to the rear, and to the surgeon's care, and then Uncle Quince stumbled himself from his own sore wound, and fell, when old master was safe. Here it was again in Central Africa, as it had been in Virginia, the same dumb, unquestioning loyalty, the same blind fidelity even unto death. As I stood over that severed limb, I saw the African's people in that other land standing faithful at the plough, while old master was away at the war, that same black arm keeping the wolf from old missus's door; I saw the African's arm, as it had borne the Cross, when the fainting

Saviour could bear it no more; and here it was again, lying all torn and gashed on that blood-stained shore, mute witness to the heroic fidelity with which they all had perished. But for me, may Almighty God forget my people and me, when I forget them and theirs!"

Col. Henry Watterson, the famous Louisville editor, delivered a brilliant speech in Carnegie Hall, New York, in the interest of Tuskegee Institute—Booker Washington's school. His subject was, "The Future of the Negro." From that speech I quote as follows:

"Nobody can go to Tuskegee, and see what I saw there, and come away without being impressed. Ever since I went there, now many years ago, I have been filled with hope; for though the institution of African slavery be dead, and, thank the Lord of Hosts for that, the negro is here; he is here in ever-increasing numbers, and he is here to stay. All schemes for getting rid of him are fantastic, and, if attempted, would prove abortive. He must be developed on new lines, educated to an anomalous situation and resolved into the body of society, not as an irritant, but as a natural, indispensable component part.

"I want nothing for myself, or for my children, which I am not ready to give to my colored neighbor and his children. I live in a region peopled by many blacks, good, orderly, hard-working folk. They know me, and they know that when I declare this I mean it. We have had no race war or serious racial conflict in Kentucky. The feudists of the mountains, the night riders of the tobacco belt, are all whites, not blacks. Reasonable white people and reasonable black people find it easy to get along much as if there existed no color line. Each is inspired by a sense of duty to the other, which, under the benign influence of religion and humanity, may yet blossom into the old domestic relations of confidence and affection, the man-ownership clause succeeded by a manhood clause, at once self-respecting and reciprocally respected.

"As, during the sectional war, they were faithful servants, remaining at home, and tilling the fields and taking care of the women and children, so, since the war, according to their lights they have tried to be good citizens. I glory in every step of progress they have made—and they have made many strides—from that day to this.

"I stand here tonight to declare that the world has never withnessed such progress from darkness to light as that which we see in those districts of the South where the negro has had a decent opportunity for self-improvement. Nowhere on the habitable globe has the liberated slave fared so well, nowhere has he so fair an outlook as in the Southern States of North America.

"Why? Because we know one another, and because, no matter what anybody may say to the contrary, there is a common bond of association between us. Never can the white man of the South forget what the black man did during the war waged for his freedom, and what he might have done. Never should the black man of the South forget that he is the weaker in the race, and for a long time to come must look to the white man for help of many kinds. It is through these reciprocal obligations and interests that the two races will reach some institutional system of living and doing entirely satisfactory to both.

"The negro in Africa has scarcely burst the chrysalis of the primitive state of man. In America he is yet in a state of racial childhood. As he realizes this, the faster he will grow, the quicker he will learn, and the sooner he will reach his racial manhood. In less than half a century he has achieved wonders. Before the century we have just begun is half over he will have achieved greater still. He has yet, and upon an extensive scale, to learn habits of method and order; habits of tenacity and acquisition; habits of sustained industry and sobriety, without which no race—white, red, brown, or black—or any individual man—can get on and prosper.

"He is a bad white man who will not help his neighbor black man, when that neighbor black man shows the spirit to help himself. He is a bad black man who cherishes hatred in his heart against the white man because he is a white man. He is a foolish black man who thinks because the mirage of social equality, which would prove a curse rather than a blessing, is denied him, that the white man hates him. Social questions the world over create their own laws and settle themselves. They can not be forced. It is idle anywhere for anybody to contest or quarrel with them. No man should wish to go where he is not wanted; true, self-respecting men dismiss the very thought of it, going their own way, hoeing their own row, and giving praise to God that their happiness is within themselves, and beyond the reach of any man, be he white or black, king or vassal."

The Rev. Alexander Sprunt, D. D., pastor of the First Presbyterian church of Charleston, preached an able sermon to his congregation on December 1, 1907. His subject was, "Give the Negro the Gospel," and he took for his text the words, "For the Jews have no dealings with the Samaritans." Dr. Sprunt belongs to the Southern Presbyterian Church, and we may take it for granted that in this sermon he voiced the sentiments of that great denomination of Christians. He said, in part:

"The general assembly of the Presbyterian Church in the United States, commonly known as the Southern Presbyterian Church, appoints an annual collection to be taken on the first Sabbath in December for the evangelization of the colored people of our Southland. There are some who are very much prejudiced against this cause, because they have no dealings with the negro, and no sympathy for the work. They would rather give to almost anything else. Let us see, 'the Jews had no dealings with the Samaritans.'

"Now and then some white man maintains that the black man has no soul. As well doubt the existence of the soul altogether. The Holy Ghost says, 'God hath made of one blood all nations of men for to dwell on all the face of the earth, and hath determined the times before appointed, and the bounds of their habitation; that they should seek the Lord, if haply they might feel after him, and find him, though he be not far from every one of us.' Acts 17:26, 27.

"Yet it is sometimes said that neither religion nor education is a benefit to the race; but such a statement carries its own contradiction. It may be that some forms of religion are no benefit to the negro, but neither are they beneficial to any others. Some kinds of education may not be helpful to them either. But these forms are not prescribed. We all know they are a very religious people, and they will have some form of religion. It is our part to give them a pure religion, and the kind of education which will elevate them, and make them the best of citizens, and most enlightened Christians. The Commissioner of Education reports to the United States government that 'from both a moral and religious point of view, what measure of education the negro has received has paid and there has been no backward step in any State. Not a single graduate of Hampton Institute or of the Tuskegee Institute can be found today in any jail or State penitentiary. The record of the South shows that 90 per cent. of the colored people in prison are without a knowledge of trades, and 61 per cent. are illiterate.' In 1865 only a very small proportion of the negroes of the South could read. Today not less than 30,000 are professors and teachers in schools and colleges. A vast number of well-read preachers, lawyers, doctors, mail agents and clerks are at work today. There are more than 150 newspapers edited by negroes. The percentage of illiteracy has fallen from 70 per cent. in 1880 to 56 per cent. in 1890, and to 44 per cent. in 1900.

"This race is susceptible to wholesome religious training and useful education. It is ours to give it to them. They have a right to the Gospel of our Lord Jesus as much as we have. What right have any of us to it? It is ours in possession by the grace of God, but not ours to hoard or keep to ourselves, but it is ours in trust.

"These people are our neighbors, and the 'second great commandment' leaves us no liberty whatever in our obligations to them.

"If, then, they are in such need, are susceptible of the glorious benefits of the Gospel; if they have a right to it, and are our neighbors, and we have it to give them, surely it is our duty to give it to them and to do so at once."

In these two articles, I have given a few expressions from representative Southern white people for the negro. But there are white people like these scattered all over the South. They are a brave, courageous, and Christ-like band.

IX.

The White People's Care of the Old Black Mammies.

The care that the Southern white people take of the old black mammy is a sign of a better day for the negro in the South.

The old black mammy of ante-bellum days did not pass away with the passing of that period. And it is predicted that it is likely that they will never cease to be in the South. It is a system that is likely to spread to the North. There is a mutual confidence and love that naturally springs up between the colored cook, nurse or maid on the one hand and the white people on the other, let them be Southern or Northern white folks. There are thousands of black mammies in the South today who have almost the entire charge of the children of some of the best white families. Not only are the life and health of these children in their hands, but the moral and spiritual training of the little ones likewise. And these children are not all motherless children, either—in fact, very few of them are motherless. Their parents are living, but because of the faith and confidence they have in mammy's integrity and religion, they turn the little ones over to her. She is hired to care for their bodies, but she does not neglect their other natures. And among other things that she teaches them she teaches them good manners. The molding hand of the old black mammy tells on the life of the child through all its future career, and even into the life beyond.

For all this work the old black mammy is paid her wages. And when the infirmities of old age come on and she is not able to work any more she is often granted a pension by her white folks, or given a room in their house or yard, and fed from their table. In sickness the best medical attention is given at their expense, and often the white ladies take their turn at watching and do part of the nursing. Mammy's pastor and her church brothers and sisters are not forbidden to see her. And when death comes and mammy is dead, the white folks bury her—paying all funeral expenses, and frequently attend the funeral at the church. Such cases happen throughout the South. I will give two or three instances.

At Lake City, S. C., there is a white gentleman —Mr. S. M. Askins—who had an old colored woman who lived in his family for thirty years. She raised his two children—Hoxie and Willie. The old woman's name was Lozetta McFadden. Mr. Askins gave her a very nice and comfortable home. He gave her titles for the land and built her a good house. He did this as a reward for her faithfulness, and instructed his children that they must never allow her to want for anything while she lived. The children have carefully obeyed their father's instructions. Mammy Lozetta has always been considered as a member of the Askins family, and does not hesitate to draw on them whenever in need. And her requests for assistance are never denied.

There is a very touching case of this nature that came under the writer's own observation in the city of Charleston. When he was pastor of Old Bethel M. E. Church there was an old blind sister connected with that congregation whose name was Hagar Seabrook. She lived in the yard of the late Mr. Holmes on Charlotte street, the East Bay oil and paint merchant. The old sister told the writer that she raised Mrs. Holmes, the merchant's wife, and then assisted her in raising her children. She was the cook and nurse, and when she became old and blind, Mrs. Holmes gave her a comfortable room in her yard. All the wood she needed for fire was given to her. It was cut, split and carried to her room. Her meals were sent to her three times a day and she told this writer that she ate just what the white folks ate. All the servants in the yard were instructed to look after mammy and do for her whatever she wanted done. Every Sunday afternoon one of the young ladies of the house—one of Mrs. Holmes' daughters—would go to mammy's room and spend hours with her reading the Bible for her. And when the family would go to the mountains to spend the summer, Mrs. Holmes and her daughters would write some very beautiful, touching and consoling letters to mammy. Many of these letters were read by the writer on the occasion when he would be making a pastoral visit to "Mother Seabrook," as she was affectionately called by her church people.

But, by and by, the old soul was paralyzed, but Mrs. Holmes did not forsake her. Though she was blind and helpless from paralysis, Mrs. Holmes stood by her and cared for her to the last. And when she died, Mrs. Holmes sent for a colored undertaker and told him to give mammy a respectable burial and send the bill to her. This was done, and the writer, assisted by the late Rev. Dr. J. H. Welch, who was at that time pastor of the Emmanuel A. M. E. Church, performed the burial services, Mrs. Holmes and her daughters being present. There are thousands of cases just like this in all parts of the South.

I clipped the following touching incident from the American Magazine. It was written by Mr. Ray Stannard Baker just after the Atlanta riot. He says: "The mass of colored people still maintain, as I have said, a more or less intimate connection with white families, frequently a very beautiful and sympathetic relationship like that of the old mammies or nurses. To one who has heard so much of racial hatred as I have since I have been down here, a little incident that I observed the other day comes with a charm hardly describable. I saw a carriage stop in front of a home. The expected daughter had arrived—a very pretty girl indeed. She stepped out eagerly. Her father was half way down to the gate, but ahead of him was a very old negro woman in the cleanest of clean starched dresses.

"'Honey,' she said eagerly. 'Mammy!' exclaimed the girl, and the two rushed into each others' arms, clasping and kissing, the white girl and the old black woman.

"I thought to myself: 'There's no negro problem there: that's just plain human love.'"

When Senator James Gordon, of Mississippi, was leaving the United States Senate not long since he read an original poem entitled, "The Old Black Mammy." I herewith reproduce it:

THE OLD BLACK MAMMY.

'Tis easy to wander off from my theme
  When traveling over the ground;
Thro' evergreen pastures across the bright
    stream
  When in fancy I wander around,
And see in the picture which never grows older
Tho' age chills the blood which never grows
    colder.

In fancy I see those good old negroes again
  I loved in the days long ago,
As they worked in the fields of cotton and grain
  And sung as they chopped with the hoe;
I can never forget, wherever I roam,
The scenes of my childhood and home.

The dear old black mammy, so gentle and tender,
  So faithful and true to her trust—
I loved her so well I dared not offend her;
  She is gone, yet I honor her dust.
From the wells of my heart arise tears of regret;
Tho' she sleeps 'neath the sod, I can never forget.

She was lovely to me in her colored bandanna
  With which she turbaned her head;
Her songs were far sweeter than flute or piano
  As she put me to sleep in my bed;
Her soft, crooning voice I can never forget,
Like an angel, in dreams, she comes to me yet.

A few years ago I clipped the following from the New York World:

A SOUTHERN WOMAN'S PROTEST.

To the Editor of The World:

Tired of the continual warfare upon the colored race, I, a Southern woman, vigorously shout my protest. Accustomed to their kindly faces from childhood, I fling my praise. The negro pleads for justice. He does not crave equality. They are grateful, trusting and sympathetic. As to their patience, it reaches the sublime. They exist against fearful odds, "Put yourself in his place." Heinous crimes are committed only by the ignorant, hunted, starved desperado. Such creatures frequently degrade every nationality. For every rascally negro (I am unbiased) score tenfold white demons, the majority arrayed in fine cloth. Day and night they await every opportunity (base human vultures, fair-skinned) to drag innocent girl victims in the meshes of gilded vice. Lavish expenditure on wines, blandishments, deceit are unblushingly used as a means to success. No man can gainsay me. Remove the causes.

Stop this un-Christian crusade against the poor, downtrodden black man and educate the "white boss" to show him a better example. Faithfully, I was rocked on the breast of a saintly old black mammy in my babyhood. Today her memory I still revere. I can not resist defending her helpless race. Far better give him a chance to earn his living than to despise and execute without lawful sanction.

LOUISIANA.

If there could only be more people of the same opinion, how much better the two races would get along together. There's a truth in every sentence of that person's generous letter, and we are glad that there is some one who thinks as she does about the situation.

Old Black Mammy.

(Many of the Southern States propose erecting a monument to the old black mammy of ante-bellum days.—Daily Paper.)

Away down South in Dixieland
  Where snowy fields of cotton grow,
And live-oaks stand in mossy cloaks
  Like ghostly soldiers in a row,
And banjos tinkle to the moon,
  And winds are heavy with the scent
Of jasmine and magnolias,
  They want to raise a monument
    To old black mammy.

The memory of her ebon face
  Beneath its scarlet turban gay,
Is dear to all her babies yet,
  Though they are wrinkled, bent and gray.
She rocked them in her loving arms,
  And crooned them off to happy rest,
And all their childish griefs and pains
  Were soothed upon the ample breast
    Of old black mammy.

She peopled with her fancy quaint
  Each bush and tree with spectres bold,
And while a son of Dixie lives
  Her folk-lore stories will be told.
They dwell in every Southern heart,
  They roll from every Southern tongue,
The mystic, droll, romantic tales
  Her children loved to hear when young
    From old black mammy.

Her loyal faith in things divine,
  Her simple creed of hope and trust,
Survive the seasons as they fade,
  And rise triumphant from the dust.
Her skin was black, her soul was white,
  Her many virtues justly claim
The tribute of a sculptured stone
  To glorify the lowly name
    Of old black mammy.

MINA IRVING, McGirt's Magazine.